Recovering Autism, ADHD, and Special Needs

Author and Illustrator:

Shelley Tzorfas

Developmental Editor:
Salvatore Canzonieri

D1607158

1

Publisher
In a Shell Publications

Author
Shelley Tzorfas

Developmental Editor
Salvatore Canzonieri

Publication Design
BGT ENT

Cover Design and Illustrations
Shelley Tzorfas

Recovering Autism, ADHD, and Special Needs

published by
In a Shell Publications
2317 Gates Court
Morris Plains, NJ 07950

www.betterschoolresults.com

First edition January 2013
ISBN-10: 0988853108
ISBN-13: 979-0-9888531-0-2

10 9 8 7 6 5 4 3 2 1

Printed in USA

ACKNOWLEDGMENTS

The author would like to give special thanks to my friend Salvatore Canzonieri for his efforts in proofreading and editing this book. His help in organizing and developing the content as Developmental Editor has been invaluable. His vast knowledge of the subject matter and his experience in healing work added dimensions and insights that were hard to put in words. Not only were his skills appreciated but he was proactive in his support of my completing the project, with unwavering belief in its success.

I also thank the following people for their assistance: Denis of Water Planet, Jamie Grover of *Autism on the Seas*, Stephen Muller and the staff of Landmark College, and John M. Hutchinson, PhD, Interim President and other staff over at Beacon College. The author would also like to thank Caroline Janover, Roman Bystrianyk, Barbara Loe Fisher, the co-founder and president of the National Vaccine Information Center (NVIC), and Ginger Taylor, the Executive Director of the Canary Party.

Introduction

Four decades ago, it was promised by the medical establishment that the United States would strive to cure cancer, diabetes, and other illnesses that have long plagued our society. In the current era of medical research, we have been asked to "walk" for these cures. We walk for Autism; we walk for Diabetes; we walk for Breast Cancer; Prostate Cancer; and all of the other diseases that affect those we love. Where has all this walking gotten us? More money going to the pharmaceutical companies, who in turn make more medicines and vaccines that cause more forms of cancer, Autism and Diabetes. Where has that really gotten us? It has gotten us to "walking in circles." Science without conscience.

In this book I promote no product. I have no hidden agenda to make money for any pharmaceutical company, nutritional style, or recovery center. I do not make money when I ask you to take vitamin supplements or see certain doctors. This book was written solely to help you recover your child and to make the lives of children, both present and future, better. I am passionate about this work, having spent decades involved in the recovery of children. Many authors publish successfully due to their doctoral qualifications and institutional links, at times being a mere part of the job as opposed to a passion-driven process. My work exists solely to improve the health of those children with Autism, ADD, and other special needs.

This book is formatted in double columns because, as discussed in Chapter 2, it less straining on the eyes making tracking from left to right easier. People who often lose their places when reading will find that they can maintain their places with less effort.

Note: Citations and references are found at the end of this book.

Chapter 1: At the Precipice

People have become conditioned to accept a growing number of children with diagnoses such as Attention Deficit/Hyperactivity Disorder (ADHD), Autistic Spectrum Disorder (ASD), Learning Disabilities (LD), and other so-called psychiatric disorders and disabilities. In previous generations, an ill child might have been an anomaly that attracted the stares of other children and adults. Today, people can hardly go to a library, movie theater, shopping mall, park, or classroom without encountering chronically ill children that are now commonplace in current society. Ironically, the resources touted as having marvelous impacts on the health of our children are the very same resources that have created these perpetually ill children.

All mental disorders that are agreed upon amongst the psychiatric community are listed in the *Diagnostic and Statistical Manual of Mental Disorders* (DSM). There is a discrepancy as to the number of mental and psychiatric disorders enumerated in the DSM. One source states that there are 106 mental/psychiatric disorders while other sources give different numbers (DSM History, 2010; Grob, 1991). By 1994, the different mental illnesses listed in the DSM had escalated to 250 mental/psychiatric disorders.

The newest DSM will include many new disorders and it will even change the Dyslexia description. Instead, they are restructuring aspects of Dyslexia into separate disorders. For example, children who do not like mathematics may be diagnosed as having an "MD" or Mathematical Disorder. There previously existed a name for children and adults with a Mathematical Disorder, known as Dyscalculia, which was a type of Dyslexia, pertaining to numbers. In the newest DSM, it is referred to as a new disorder. I speculate that the purpose of defining this new disorder is to support an increase in new or repurposed medications. But, this condition can not be remedied via medication; it requires one on one teaching at an individual pace, which is education not medication.

The 1994 edition of the DSM-IV was 886 pages long. The newer DSM, due in 2013, will be far lengthier (Maser & Patterson, 2002). I'm hoping that the reader finds this of concern.[i]

DSM Version	Date Issued	Number of Pages	Number of Disorders
DSM-I	1952	130	106
DSM-II	1968	134	182
DSM-III	1980	494	265
DSM-IV	1994	889	297

The Toxicity of Vaccines

The author feels that Autism, ADHD, and other such disorders are not psychiatric in nature but are instead physical illnesses, most of which began from exposure to contaminates and toxins. The largest amount of toxins and harmful exposure come from items now found in vaccines such as Aluminum, Thimerosal (mercury), Ether, MSG, Embalming Fluid, Polysorbates, and other dangerous chemicals. Vaccines also contain human fetal cells and animal DNA.

Some argue that Formaldehyde can be found as well. Once injected, the toxins and contaminates bypass the body's digestive system where they would have had the chance to be neutralized somewhat rather than going directly into the bloodstream; some coagulate in the human brain.

In earlier times, a few vaccines were thought to be of great help for preventing diseases. I suppose that the human body is capable of handling a certain amount of foreign chemicals when there were only a few vaccines administrated at a time. In previous times, it was natural for a child to be exposed to childhood diseases such as chicken pox and measles. A child would have been exposed to only one or two diseases at a time within a year or so, which would not compromise their young immune systems.

Most healthy children were able to overcome childhood diseases.

But today, children get a large number of vaccinations at the same time; sometimes being injected at one time with up to 16 to 20 different antigens! This situation obviously would be very taxing on a child's still developing immune system. Further, babies today are being vaccinated right after birth, before their immune system is even fully formulated; and others are vaccinating when a woman is pregnant, before a baby is even born. Decades ago, people instead received about 5 to 10 vaccinations at the most in one lifetime.

The number of vaccinations began to greatly increase due to a law passed in 1986 called the *National Childhood Vaccine Injury Act*. This piece of legislation prevented people from suing a vaccine maker in regular courts[ii]. This made the vaccine industry the only widely held corporations in America that could not be sued in regular civil court. Instead, "Vaccine Courts" were established to make rulings, essentially giving the pharmaceutical industry immunity from the consequences of having poisonous or toxic ingredients contained in their vaccines. Few cases are heard in that court. From that time forward, children went from getting fewer than 10 vaccines by age 18 to getting up to 70 or more vaccines by 18. Today, approximately 36 vaccinations are often given before the age of two.

It has been said that a baby is born with its mother's immune system (Hanson & Silfverdal, 2009). Some claim that any vaccine given to a child before the age of six months will then be flushed out when the baby transitions from the mother's immune system to its own (Sheppard, 2008). Others claim that any vaccine will be flushed out by the baby's emerging immune system by the age of one.

Shots such as DPT, Diptheria, Pertussis (Whooping Cough), and Tetanus are given at the ages of two, four, and six months. Shots such as the MMR (Measles, Mumps, and Rubella) are administered at different intervals. Not only are these three-in-one shots dangerous for the infant or child, but often times three or four needles are given in a single doctor's visit, which contain vaccines supposedly to prevent up to 16 different diseases.

In previous generations getting so many vaccines at one time was not standard practice. The shots issued by doctors today aren't the same shots that were administered in the 60s and 70s.

Today, the adjuvant chemicals are much stronger. Under usual circumstances, the gut would be able to reduce toxicity through digestive processes before going through muscle and nerve tissue. By injecting toxins directly into the muscles and bypassing the gut altogether, these poisons often have the possibility of going directly to the brain.

Contaminates and Adjuvants

What is in these vaccines? The concept of a vaccine is that doctors take dead or weakened versions of a virus and insert it into our most active tissues, our muscle tissues, where our body proceeds to fight it off by building an immune response. That, however, is not the whole picture, although I wish it was. Instead, understand that a variety of vaccines contain contaminants, which include formaldehyde, mercury, aluminum, embalming fluid, antifreeze, aborted fetal tissue, Squalene, peanut by-products, Thimerosal, Ether, Polysorbate 80, and cells and viruses from monkeys, cows, pigs, chickens, and dogs.

Some of these materials are used as immunologic adjuvants. According to the National Cancer Institute, adjuvants are agents added to a vaccine so that it may stimulate the immune system and increase its response to a vaccine. "Adjuvants have been whimsically called the *dirty little secret* of vaccines in the scientific community. This dates from the early days of commercial vaccine manufacture, when significant variations in the effectiveness of different batches of the same vaccine were observed, correctly assumed to be due to contamination of the reaction vessels. However, it was soon found that more scrupulous attention to cleanliness actually seemed to *reduce* the effectiveness of the vaccines, and that the contaminants – "dirt" – actually enhanced the immune response. There are many known adjuvants in widespread use, including oils, aluminum salts, and virosomes." - The Scientist *"Deciphering Immunology's Dirty Secret"*, by Kate Travis; January 1, 2007.

The problem is that many of these substances are mixed together and implanted in human tissue in ways that would never have occurred in nature, creating concoctions that cause negative physical reactions, sometimes quite severe. The damage from the resultant toxic effects far outweighs the benefits that may be provided to the immune system. Even more alarming is that newborn babies have been vaccinated,

since about 1991, against a sexually transmitted disease when they are between only three hours and 12 hours old. This immunity wears off by the time the child is five. Some parents have come to believe that their child was born autistic, when many were actually injured by this vaccine on their *first* precious day of life.

NOTE: As of the time of publication, not only did the United States Vaccine Court award $2.3 billion to over 80 families who proved that vaccines injured their children. In fact more cases are currently in process. In Europe the courts have declared that vaccines cause autism, narcolepsy, and other damage to the brain.

Following is a table showing a modest sampling of foreign ingredients found in vaccines given to your newborn baby:

Foreign Ingredients Found in Vaccines - A Representative Sample				
Vaccine	Microbes	Antibiotics	Chemicals / Heavy Metals	Animal By products
Acel-Immune DTaP diphtheria - tetanus – pertussis	diphtheria and tetanus toxoids and acellular pertussis adsorbed		formaldehyde, aluminum hydroxide, aluminum phosphate, thimerosal, and polysorbate 80 (Tween-80)	Gelatin
Act HIB *Haemophilus influenza* Type B	*Haemophilus influenza* Type B, polyribosylribitol phosphate		ammonium sulfate, formalin, and sucrose	
Attenuvax Measles	measles live virus	neomycin	sorbitol	hydrolyzed gelatin, chick embryo
Biavax Rubella	rubella live virus	Neomycin	sorbitol	hydrolyzed gelatin, human diploid cells from aborted fetal tissue
BioThrax anthrax adsorbed	nonencapsulated strain of *Bacillus anthracis*		aluminum hydroxide, benzethonium chloride, and formaldehyde	

DPT diphtheria – tetanus – pertussis	diphtheria and tetanus toxoids and acellular pertussis adsorbed		formaldehyde, aluminum phosphate, ammonium sulfate, and thimerosal	washed sheep RBCs
Dryvax smallpox (not licensed d/t expiration)	live vaccinia virus, with "some microbial contaminants," according to the Working Group on Civilian Biodefense	polymyxcin B sulfate, streptomycin sulfate, chlortetracycline hydrochloride, and neomycin sulfate	glycerin, and phenol –a compound obtained by distillation of coal tar	vesicle fluid from calf skins
Engerix-B recombinant hepatitis B	genetic sequence of the hepatitis B virus that codes for the surface antigen (HbSAg), cloned into GMO yeast		aluminum hydroxide, and thimerosal	
Fluvirin	influenza virus	neomycin, polymyxin	beta-propiolactone	chick embryonic fluid
FluShield	trivalent influenza virus, types A&B	gentamicin sulphate	_olysorbates, thimerosal, and _olysorbates 80 (Tween-80)	chick embryonic fluid

Havrix hepatitis A	hepatitis A virus		formalin, aluminum hydroxide, 2-phenoxyethanol, and polysorbate 20	residual MRC5 proteins -human diploid cells from aborted fetal tissue
HiB Titer *Haemophilus influenza* Type B	*Haemophilus influenza* Type B, polyribosylribitol phosphate, yeast		ammonium sulfate, thimerosal, and chemically defined yeast-based medium	
Imovax	rabies virus adsorbed	neomycin sulfate	phenol red indicator	human albumin, diploid cells from aborted fetal tissue
IPOL	3 types of polio viruses	neomycin, streptomycin, and polymyxin B	formaldehyde, and 2-phenoxyethenol	continuous line of monkey kidney cells
JE-VAX Japanese encephalitis	*Nakayama-NIH* strain of Japanese encephalitis virus, inactivated		formaldehyde, polysorbate 80 (Tween-80), and thimerosal	mouse serum proteins, and gelatin
LYMErix Lyme	recombinant protein (OspA) from the outer surface of the spirochete *Borrelia burgdorferi*	kanamycin	aluminum hydroxide, 2-phenoxyethenol, phosphate buffered saline	

MMR measles - mumps – rubella	measles, mumps, rubella live virus	Neomycin	sorbitol	hydrolized gelatin, chick embryonic fluid, and human diploid cells from aborted fetal tissue
M-R-Vax measles - rubella	measles, rubella live virus	neomycin	sorbitol	hydrolized gelatin, chick embryonic fluid, and human diploid cells from aborted fetal tissue
Menomune meningococca	freeze-dried polysaccharide antigens from *Neisseria* *meningitidis* bacteria		thimerosal	Lactose
Meruvax I Mumps	mumps live virus	Neomycin	Sorbitol	hydrolized gelatin
NYVAC (new smallpox batch, not licensed)	highly attenuated vaccinia virus	polymyxcin B sulfate, streptomycin sulfate, chlortetracycli ne hydrochloride, and neomycin sulfate	glycerin, and phenol -a compound obtained by distillation of coal tar	vesicle fluid from calf skins

Orimune oral polio	3 types of polio viruses, attenuated	neomycin, streptomycin	Sorbitol	monkey kidney cells and calf serum
Pneumovax *Streptococcus pneumonia*	capsular polysaccharides from polyvalent (23 types) pneumococcal bacteria		Phenol	
Prevnar Pneumococcal 7-valent conjugate vaccine	saccharides from capsular *Streptococcus pneumoniae* antigens (7 serotypes) individually conjugated to diphtheria CRM $_{197}$ protein		aluminum phosphate, ammonium sulfate, soy protein, yeast	
ProQuad measles, mumps, rubella and varicella	live measles (Enders' attenuated Edmonston), mumps (Jeryl Lynn^{TM}), rubella (Wistar RA 27/3), and varicella (oka/Merck) strains of viruses	Neomycin	monosodium L-glutamate (MSG), potassium chloride, potassium phosphate monobasic, potassium phosphate dibasic, sodium bicarbonate, sodium phosphate dibasic, sorbitol, and sucrose	human albumin, human diploid cells, residual components of MRC-5 cells including DNA and proteins, bovine serum, hydrolized gelatin, and chicken embryo

RabAvert Rabies	fixed-virus strain Flury LEP	neomycin, chlortetracycline, and amphotericin B	potassium glutamate, and sucrose	human albumin, bovine gelatin & serum "from source countries known to be free of bovine spongioform encephalopathy," and chicken protein
Rabies Vaccine Adsorbed	rabies virus adsorbed		beta-propiolactone, aluminum phosphate, thimerosal, and phenol red	rhesus monkey fetal lung cells
Recombivax recombinant hepatitis B	genetic sequence of the hepatitis B virus that codes for the surface antigen (HbSAg), cloned into GMO yeast		aluminum hydroxide, and thimerosal	
RotaShield oral tetravalent rotavirus (recalled)	1 rhesus monkey rotavirus, 3 rhesus-human reassortant l ive viruses	neomycin sulfate, amphotericin B	potassium monophosphate, potassium diphosphate, sucrose, and monosodium glutamate (MSG)	rhesus monkey fetal diploid cells, and bovine fetal serum

Smallpox (not licensed due to expiration) 40-yr old stuff "found" in Swiftwater, PA freezer	live vaccinia virus, with "some microbial contaminants," according to the Working Group on Civilian Biodefense	polymyxcin B sulfate, streptomycin sulfate, chlortetracycline hydrochloride, and neomycin sulfate	glycerin, and phenol –a compound obtained by distillation of coal tar	vesicle fluid from calf skins
Smallpox (new, not licensed)	highly attenuated vaccinia virus	polymyxcin B sulfate, streptomycin sulfate, chlortetracycline hydrochloride, and neomycin sulfate	glycerin, and phenol -a compound obtained by distillation of coal tar	vesicle fluid from calf skins
TheraCys BCG (intravesicle - not licensed in US for tuberculosis)	live attenuated strain of *Mycobacterium bovis*		monosodium glutamate (MSG), and polysorbate 80 (Tween-80)	
Tripedia diphtheria - tetanus – pertussis	*Corynebacterium diphtheriae* Clostridium tetani toxoids and acellular *Bordetella pertussis* Adsorbed		aluminum potassium sulfate, formaldehyde, thimerosal, and polysorbate 80 (Tween-80)	gelatin, bovine extract US sourced

Typhim Vi Typhoid	cell surface Vi polysaccharide from *Salmonella typhi* Ty2 strain		aspartame, phenol, and polydimethylsilox ane (silicone)	
Varivax Chickenpox	varicella live virus	Neomycin	phosphate, sucrose, and monosodium glutamate (MSG)	processed gelatin, fetal bovine serum, guinea pig embryo cells, albumin from human blood
YF-VAX yellow fever	17D strain of yellow fever		sorbitol	chick embryo, and gelatin

(Table cited from website www.informedchouce.info/cocktail.html)[iii]

Many people have not thought about nor seen these charts showing the multitude of vaccines and vaccine ingredients that people are injected with. For those seeing this information for the first time, pay special attention to the Hepatitis B shot. Notice in the far right column, it has "residual MRC5 proteins - human diploid cells from aborted fetal tissue". The vaccine for Measles, Mumps, and Rubella, and Varicella contains the chemicals Monosodium L-Glutamate (MSG), Potassium Chloride, Potassium Phosphate Monobasic, Potassium Phosphate Dibasic, Sodium Bicarbonate, Sodium Phosphate Dibasic, Sorbitol and Sucrose. Besides these dangerous chemicals, it contains human albumin, human diploid cells, residual components of MRC-5 cells including DNA and proteins, bovine serum, hydrolyzed gelatin, and chicken embryo. Other vaccines contain non-kosher pork and pig products (DailyMed, 2008).

It can be seen how adverse reactions can possibly occur in newborns with newly forming immune systems that are exposed to many different chemicals and foreign proteins. This is just a small sampling of some vaccines.

Infant Strokes Post-Vaccination

For those parents out there wondering whether or not your child became ill as a result of being vaccinated, first look at photos of your baby's face when you believed your baby to be healthy. Next, compare that photo to other pictures of your baby's face after you felt that your baby suddenly lost speech or eye contact abilities, started screaming uncontrollably, or stopped sleeping through the night for more than a few consecutive days. What you might notice in the photos is that one eye turns to the side or tends to droop, the corner of the lips on one side of the face points down or up, or, more significantly, the baby's face is no longer symmetrical.[iv] All of these are significant signs of a possible stroke or a blockage of blood or oxygen to the brain, which indicates that there may be a potential relationship between these strokes and vaccines. This sudden change of face is most noticeable between the ages of 15 and 18 months old when children get their series of DPT, MMR, and HIB shots.

Why do these strokes tend to occur more frequently at this age? If we take bee sting allergies as an example, a person must usually be stung several times before developing an anaphylactic-type allergic reaction. It's not the first sting, and usually not the second, that causes these ill effects. By the third sting, however, the body fights back with such force that anaphylactic shock occurs. A similar reaction occurs with vaccine shots when the body can no longer fight the invader. A baby with a thriving immune system can suddenly withdraw as the toxic chemicals begin to attack the brain and the gut.

Signs that your baby may be having a dangerous reaction include a lump on the leg at the site of the injection, a certain high-pitched scream that may last for hours, vomiting, a high fever, or even collapsing. Consider these reactions as warnings to you, as a parent, that more of these signs are yet to come. In retrospect, some parents can remember phoning their physicians only to hear, "fever is common after injection, just give your baby Motrin or Tylenol," when in reality fever is a reaction that can help the child burn off harmful chemicals, toxic substances, and/or infections from the body. By lowering the fever you may thwart your child's ability to fight off the invaders.

Diseases Declining Before Vaccinations

Research has shown that many diseases began to decline and even practically disappear before any vaccinations were introduced for them OR even when there was no vaccine available. Many factors had and have majorly influenced the natural decline or disappearance of contagious diseases.

These factor include more efficient and effective methods of:

• Sanitation (clean water, air, food, and a clean environment.);

- Water and sewage treatment;

- Public health departments and regulations;

- Personal bathing / Hygiene;

- Quality nutrition, all year around, not just seasonal;

- Pest control;

- Quarantine.

Throughout most of history, conditions in many towns, cities, and countries were filthy, with a lack of proper sanitation and contamination of water and other resources. It was not even understood that germs caused disease. But during the mid 1800's, it was finally proven that there was a connection between germs and diseases. Soon after, cleansing agents such as soaps and disinfectants began to be developed and put to use as it was recognized that diseases could be controlled.

The following charts show how the mortality of diseases began to decline even before the advent of vaccines.

Note: No vaccine was ever created for Scarlet Fever, which virtually disappeared. Also, no widespread vaccination was ever used for Typhoid Fever.

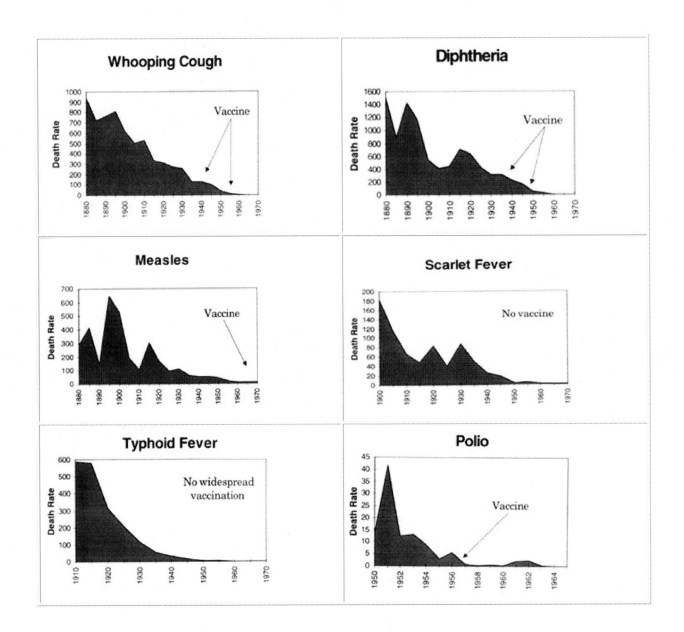

Mortality Graphs

From: _Vaccination, A Parents Dilemma_, Greg Beattle, c 1997, Oracle Press,

Queensland, Australia, p. 36-57.

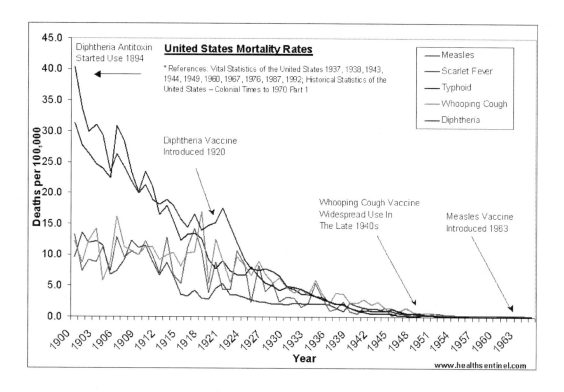

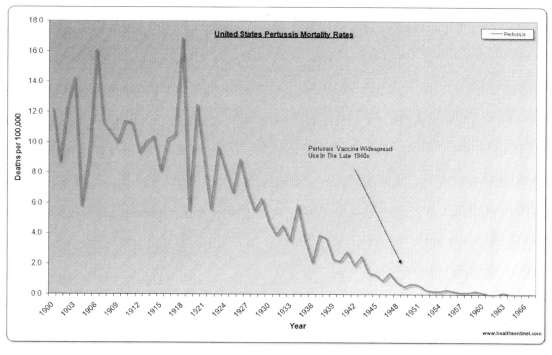

– Charts Published: Roman Bystrianyk

It is important to be informed about your legal right to vaccinate or *not* vaccinate. Nearly every state in the United States offers a legal route for parents to receive a vaccine exemption, i.e., religious exemption, which is available in most states. Currently, around 20 states offer philosophical exemptions to vaccination (in other words, it is against your belief system to expose your child to the vaccine ingredients and harmful vaccines themselves).

In posting the following Vaccine Exemption Chart by the National Vaccine Information Center (NVIC), headquartered in Virginia, it is of the utmost importance to understand that the chart is fluid; it can change on a regular basis. For example, Vermont currently (at the time of publication) has philosophical exemptions, religious exemptions, and medical exemptions available. However, there is a push to remove some of the state's available exemptions, which has resulted in a backlash from non-political parents who are trying to keep their exemptions intact. The same is happening in California. As of right now, California has medical and philosophical exemptions. Pharmaceutical interest groups often lobby the legislation, creating a pattern of exemptions being taken away and re-offered.

It would seem that your strongest type of exemption would be that of a medical nature; for example, your child may have a nut allergy that may prohibit the further use of vaccines. Your child might have cancer, which greatly weakens his or her immune system. Unfortunately, more often than not, the parent gets a temporary medical exemption and the government perpetually makes you have to prove from year to year that your child is still ill and will suffer a consequence. Proving that your child could become ill from a vaccine means a doctor must sign a statement. Finding a doctor willing to sign such a statement is difficult, but to perpetually have them re-sign is even more difficult. Having to prove yourself time and again is difficult when the state is positioned that the vaccines are good and are in your family's best interest.

Vaccination Exemption Chart

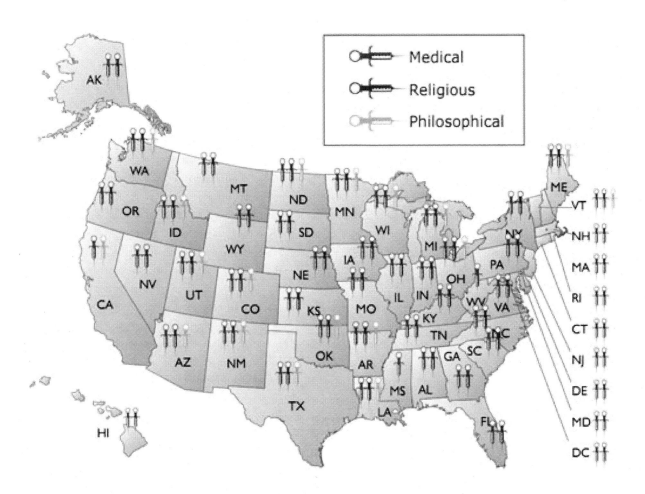

Vaccination Issues

When young, nearly every moment for a severely autistic child is a "therapeutic moment." An example is when your 18-20 month-old boy is not speaking in three-word sentences, you will often hear, "Relax," "He's a boy. Boys speak later than girls." "Don't worry about it, it will fix itself!" You'll hear this from your in-laws, on the playground, and from your neighbors; it is all well intentioned but often incorrect in today's world.

There are certainly generational differences that we can trace back to a time when newborn babies did not receive vaccinations to a time where 3-12 hour infants began receiving vaccinations. Even pregnant mothers are being given flu shots and DPT shots, how sad! In 2012, the Human and Environmental Toxicology Journal published Dr. Gary Goldman's study that shows a 4,250% increase in the number of miscarriages and stillbirths due to vaccines during the flu season. Meanwhile the CDC has recommended the double dosing of pregnant women with the seasonal flu vaccine, containing mercury and the untested H1N1 vaccine with mercury. Dr. Goldman found this situation disturbing since the safety and effectiveness of administering two different flu vaccines had never been tested on pregnant women at all. Furthermore, the vaccine manufacturers' inserts declared that it is not known if these vaccines can cause fetal harm when given to pregnant women.

That is where I am delineating the differences between the generation's health statuses. As an example, according to Mercola.com, "Hepatitis B vaccination has been recommended by federal health officials since 1991 for all infants and children." Dr. Mercola continues with, "Three hepatitis B shots are part of the standard government-recommended childhood vaccination schedule, with the first dose given at 12 hours of age in the newborn nursery of most hospitals" (Mercola, 2010).

Also, according to the Center for Disease Control (CDC), "The Centers for Disease Control and Prevention estimates that 1 in 88 children in the United States has been identified as having an Autism Spectrum Disorder (ASD), according to a new study released today that looked at data from 14 communities. Autism spectrum disorders are almost five times more common among boys than girls – with 1 in 54 boys identified" (CDC Division of News Electronic Media , 2012). Studies were based on children

born in the year 2000 and turned 8-years-old in 2008. Today, these children are 12-years-old; the studies have a 4-year lag and they did not look at children under the age of 12. It is speculated that if they looked at 3-, 4-, and 5-year-olds, the rate would be higher.

Chapter 2: Autism, What's Really Going on in There?

Changing the Criteria

The DSM contains a listing of mental/ psychiatric disorders and diagnostic criteria. In other words, it is the go-to resource for professionals. It is remarkable how many mental and psychiatric disorders there are in the DSM, especially those dealing with young children. For example, as stated previously in Chapter 1, a new mental/psychiatric disorder is to be used for labeling children who do not like math, known as MD, or Mathematical Disorder (Whitaker, 2011). This is disconcerting. The only reason I can think of for labeling children with this disorder is in order to open the door for potentially more medication. I surely would have had this label assigned to me in my childhood, but thankfully I was not born in this time period. What I have does not open the door for medication. I have Dyslexia and also Dyscalculia, which is a difficulty in understanding numbers, learning how to manipulate numbers, learning Math facts, and other related symptoms.

Autism is listed as a mental disorder in the DSM. Autism is often defined as being a neural development disorder that is characterized by impaired social interaction and communication, and also characterized by restricted and repetitive behavior. I am taking a stand that Autism is a physical, not a psychiatric or mental, illness, and it is comprised of up to 50 ailments layered on top of each other, causing physical pain. It is not really a mental or psychiatric problem as so many medical doctors, psychologists, and psychiatrists would have you believe.

When discussing the increase in the past two decades of the diagnoses of Autism, we cannot take anything for granted. Even the simple mathematics that exists in all other fields does not necessarily exist when reading about Autism. For example, a large number of articles, studies, and journals to this very day site that Autism affects one out of 166 children. There are other periodicals that are quoted as saying one of every 150. New Jersey Governor Christie in NJ in 2010 quoted that it is one in every 94 children. In early 2011, a study that was done from three different locations, when countries such as Korea were looked at it was found in one in 38 children which shocked scientists around the world. As of March 2012, the numbers are officially (via CDC) one out of every 88 children. In certain states in United States, such as Minnesota and Wisconsin, it is declared as being one in every 60 children. Reports now show that one in 54 boys are Autistic: almost a 1000% increase since 1980. Others report a different percentage of increase. So how can we rely on these so-called scientific studies when they can't accurately define not only what Autism itself is but what its prevalence is?

The discrepancy between reports presents a hodgepodge of subclinical thinking. This is a much larger issue than just an opinion. For many years, the DSM has spent decades defining a range of autistic illnesses, what they are, as well as how they're similar and different from each other. So there are terms such as HFA (High Functioning Autism), Asperger's Syndrome (for the particularly bright with little to no social skills), PDDNOS (Pervasive Developmental Disability Not

Otherwise Specified), down to classic Kanner's Autism, which was defined and written about in the early 1940s. The desluation of Autism includes: children who cannot speak, make no eye contact, bang their head, self-injure, or get lost in their own world. Years were spent identifying these categories, only to suddenly choose to remove these same categories in the DSM. Instead the scientists and psychiatrists now lump everybody together, whether your child has Albert Einstein-like tendencies or rocks back and forth while vomiting, they are all called "Autism." Conceptually, to me, it appears as if they are trying to get people to believe that Autistics are not really unusual, just part of the general population. They are trying to condition everybody to accept Autism as a fact of life. I totally disagree.

It is obvious then, rather than arguing about what Autism is and how many are afflicted, it would be much more beneficial to focus on recovery. By carefully and observantly studying a child's individual set of symptoms, you can start to find points where recovery can be achieved. I am looking for the parent or medical professional to become the Sherlock Holmes detective of their child's Autism or ADHD in assessing their child's illness. In other words, I want you to start from scratch to take a look at your child's symptoms with a magnifying glass and take nothing for granted.

The following sections explore the various symptoms of Autism and what can be done for recovery.

Sensory Overload

Imagine if you will that most of the children with moderate to severe Autism have a breakdown in the five senses: seeing, hearing, smelling, tasting, and touching. On top of that, they have peculiar sensory overload. Some Autistic children are reactive when you try to touch them, talk to them, and comfort them; others are reactive to foods. When the senses are overloaded, it means the eyes see too much – little details that most of us would ignore. At the same time, the ears hear too much, e.g., the subtle sound of the refrigerator motor, which could sound like a foghorn blasting in their ears and might prevent normal conversation and basic concentration.

These children have trouble differentiating between foreground noise and background noise. Meanwhile, their sense of smell is uncanny, almost animalistic. An example would be if the child's Aunt had perfume on when she walked into your child's bedroom to kiss him or her goodnight, causing fear in the child who could smell the perfume for the following three days in their bedroom. These types of children can also smell electricity, chemicals, and plastics.

You will notice a lot of children who have Autism (or even ADHD) like to be in small, dark, confined spaces. These are the same kinds of children who like to build tents out of their beds or who cover tables with blankets and hide under them the majority of the time. They build all kinds of forts. These autistic children are distressed; they can often hide under their bed, or hide on the bottom of their closet. Do not try to pull them out. There is a reason for them to hide the way they do. It

34

is a healthy act of self-medicating. By hiding in the dark closet, they are beginning to properly control their environment and sensory overload. They are reducing the overwhelming amounts of light, sound, and space to smaller, more manageable sizes. I prefer to encourage this behavior, working with it until the child no longer requires it. Right now they need to be in dark confined spaces to reduce the intensity of their senses.

Dr. Temple Grandin was born on August 29, 1947 and was one of the few severely autistic children growing up in the 1950s. She had been diagnosed with Autism at the age of 3 in 1950. Luckily, she started out in a structured nursery school, which was helpful to her, and speech therapy was advised. By the time Temple was 6-years-old and in first grade, she had already been suspended from various elementary schools. Despite being bullied and harassed, she got her Masters Degree in Animal Science from Arizona State University in 1975 and her Doctorate from the University of Illinois in 1989. Temple considers herself to have been lucky to have supportive mentors throughout her life.

During her childhood, her mother was adamant that Temple be exposed to as many normal situations as possible. One day, Temple's mother sent her to stay with a relative on a farm. Temple observed that many of the livestock were kicking and screaming or appeared disruptive. When the animal was placed in its pen, it would immediately calm down. She noticed that the pen was often a very small space. Temple remembers the anxiety and feeling of being threatened, made fun of, and scared of her surroundings. Perhaps because of her hypersensitivity to sound, noise, and the environment, plus her adeptness at seeing things visually in her mind, she was able to understand the fear and pain of animals in her environment and create calm, soothing spaces and ramps for animals. Temple, like so many autistic children, felt the need to be confined to a very small space or under heavy blankets, weighted vests, or dark spaces. She realized that in some ways, she felt like the animals. At this point, Grandin decided that she was going to develop a "squeeze machine." (Grandin & Scariano, 1996)

I have heard that quite a few autistic children ask for a "squeeze machine." I have seen autistic children design and invent their own practical squeeze machines. When an autistic child suddenly has a temper tantrum or an anxiety attack, they would be permitted to run into their squeeze machine, which would calm them down. Sometimes, the best place for the squeeze machine is where the child decides where he or she feels most comfortable. This physical object can take the place of medication in some children. In time, when the child learns that it is safe for them to go to the squeeze machine, the need for it will decrease and eventually disappear. They are alleviating their stresses in this manner until they feel they no longer require it.

You must understand that, at first, providing a squeeze machine can appear embarrassing or unusual to other people. People might comment, "You're letting YOUR child go in there?" They will think that you are weird. It will appear as if you are handicapping your child, but the end result of providing a squeeze machine space is that your child will eventually no longer need this type of tool.

A "squeeze machine" does what your children are already doing when they hide in a small, dark space. I would like to take it one step further than this. I recommend that you obtain a cardboard box from an appliance store and allow your child to put pillows and blankets inside for them to comfortably crawl into. Even better, if there is a small space available, allow them to put the cardboard box on the floor so that they can crawl into it in total darkness. Make sure they are choosing this space by their own volition. Once the children know that they have this very special and safe place to go to, often their need for it will diminish over time. Many good interventions are ones that quietly disappear. While at first it can seem like a handicapping crutch,

eventually the need for the crutch will disappear.

Touch Sensitivity

One of the most common symptoms of skin issues for those with Autistic Spectrum Disorder (ASD) is a propensity for the skin to become both highly sensitive and/or painful due to the various conditions that may arise. The skin is the *largest* organ in the human body, making it a very big issue to deal with when it hurts. Touch is a difficult sense to deal with in children with physical issues. Sometimes if you go to gently touch their arm, it could feel as if they were hit with a hammer, and other times when they go to touch someone in a friendly manner, it's as if *they* are hitting the other person with a ton of bricks. There is very little balance, and just like some of these kids will choose to wear a coat in the warmth of the summer, their ability to monitor their sense of touch is way off both in giving and receiving. Their sense of touch is deregulated. Sometimes these children will accidentally hurt themselves jumping off six-foot slides in a playground and will appear perfectly fine without complaining, but on the other hand will cry in pain if your fingernail gently grazes their skin. Where they should feel pain, they feel none, and when they shouldn't feel pain, they react poorly.

These children seem to sense far more than what the average person can. Children have been known to rip their clothes from their bodies due to the discomfort experienced. In cases where children are perpetually ripping off their clothes, the information that the child is giving you is, "The clothes are hurting me.

They are rubbing against my painful skin and the tag at my shirt collar feels like a razor scratching at my back." Wearing certain clothes can feel like sandpaper rubbing on such a child's skin. Tags on shirt collars can cause agony.

Sometimes it is the texture of the clothing and sometimes it is the chemicals with which the clothes are treated. The fireproofing required by law in everything from infant pajamas to furniture also affects these children due to its chemical toxicity. Somehow, incomprehensibly, fabric coloring seems as if it causes pain as well. Some kids will also notice the smell of the fabric, which can be bothersome. It is important to dust the house regularly as the chemicals from the fabric or furniture accumulates in household dust.

What makes this touch sensitivity odder is that the children do not regulate temperature well: You can find a child wanting to wear a jacket in the heat of the summer while running outside in a t-shirt during a snowstorm. This phenomenon makes no sense to you and me, but it does make sense to the individual child. How sad it is to watch other people judge the family or parent of an autistic child by saying things like, "No wonder that boy is so wild, look at how they dress him! They let him run around in a t-shirt in the winter!" Short of padlocking your front door, there is almost nothing you can do to prevent this. One day, the need to run outside without their clothes will disappear, given the right therapeutic support.

There are other skin issues that can occur as well such as a child developing red blotches of skin on their face near the lips. These blotches tend to last throughout cold winter months. It sometimes appears as if the child's own saliva is burning their skin or causing a rash, as these children tend to drool a lot, which could be possibly connected to a cow milk/soy sensitivity or allergy as well.

A number of autistic kids have skin bruises and/or cuts that may appear as if someone else did them, but in actuality they are self inflicted. Some doctors or social workers fail to acknowledge the occurrence of such self inflicted injuries amongst autistic children; they instead often diagnose the parents – usually the mother – as having Munchausen by Proxy. Munchausen by Proxy is a psychological disorder where people start to harm their children on purpose for attention. A child might be hurt on purpose; they then take their kid to a hospital. A few weeks later, the mother (and it's almost always the mother) might try other ways of hurting their child in this morbid attempt to gain attention for herself.

In many cases, parents of autistic children with hyper sensitivity are often mistakenly charged with child abuse or worse. Further, due to a lack of knowledge of the range of autistic children's oversensitivity, not only do some doctors or social workers make false allegations of Munchausen by Proxy but they also overlook or deny the fact that after vaccination deadly reactions can occur. Infants may have severe reactions to a recent vaccination, in which case the eye sockets can turn black and blue, appearing as if the infant had been shook or punched. Some babies have seizures or develop "failure to thrive" disorders. Even worse, some babies die from the day of vaccination or within four weeks. The chemicals in a vaccine sometimes cause the brain stem to swell – as in Encephalitis. Have you noticed the sharp increase of young people having seizures? The medical community is quick to point the finger at the parents, rather than do a full investigation.

Taste Sensitivity

Autistic children's sense of taste is particularly troublesome. Their sense of taste connects to their ability or inability to eat a meal, and many of the moderate-to-severely autistic kids can barely eat three or four different kinds of foods. Their diet often consists of chicken nuggets, French fries, juice, and maybe a fruit such as an apple. Other people become terribly judgmental of the families; you can often hear them say, "No wonder that kid's the way he is, look at what the family feeds him!" What the onlookers do not understand is that there is almost nothing a parent can do to change what the child will eat until that "magical moment" when the child is ready. All of a sudden the body and gut can handle a specific food because it has matured at a precise moment to be able to digest that food.

If you try to handle things as behavioral problems, forcing them to eat healthy foods by using reverse psychology, saying "Well, if you don't eat the foods I prepared for dinner then you will eat nothing," you will be surprised that these kids can and are willing to starve. Some of them will even become anorexic. I wonder, in retrospect, how many of severely anorexic kids had a form of undiagnosed Autism to begin with.

These kids vomit when you try to get healthy foods into them; they cannot handle the texture of many foods. They cannot eat the foods if they are too mushy, too crunchy, too green, or they don't like the way the food feels in their fingers. Sometimes it even goes to the extreme where the color of the plate that the food sat on has an effect on the child.

Many of these children eat mostly with their fingers. It will take years before they are willing and able to hold utensils properly. Let's not forget that many of these children have tactile sensitivities to begin with. I would like to point out that your need to have the child eat a healthy, balanced meal is more of *your* problem than it is a child's problem. Most of these children will all of a sudden start to eat healthy on their own. An example is if you were to try to make your child eat broccoli on a weekly or monthly basis, after five or six years you kind of give up on the idea altogether. One day, your friend might have your child over while you run an errand, and your child will come home and say, "I ate broccoli at Tim's house! How come you never gave me broccoli?" There are many young children who are picky, finicky eaters who are not autistic, but many autistic children have a form of this.

"Bad" Behavior

As stated previously, Autism, and also ADHD and other illnesses, are symptoms of *physical* illness, not mental or psychiatric disorders. The DSM leads us to believe that Autism is indeed a problem of a mental or psychiatric nature, followed by disruptive behaviors. The various odd actions of Autistic children can be irritating to parents or caregivers;

especially if they don't fully realize that their children have Autism. Parents see such things as children obsessively lining up all their toys day after day, demanding things to be exactly as they wish, or sitting in a corner rocking back and forth, as behavior and discipline problems. It is my experience in working with such children that these disruptive behaviors exist because the children are hurting or are troubled, and they do not occur to oppose your parental authority. Often, the child is experiencing some form of sensory discomfort or pain and finds comfort in controlling their environment.

Autistic children's seemingly bad behavior is often the result of the perpetual physical pain that they are experiencing. What appears to be a simple tantrum when children bang or press themselves onto furniture may in fact have non-obvious causes. Such children will thrust themselves onto the arm of a couch or the back of a chair simply because their abdomen hurts. The child almost never throws a tantrum and follows it up by saying, "Mommy, my stomach hurts." It would be excellent if they did, but that is not the reality of the situation. These children are in fact trying to provide gut pressure. They are seeking relief but do not know how to manage it.

Let's take a look at extreme cases where a child might self-mutilate, such as cutting or scratching the forearms and wrists to the point of bleeding. Sometimes the child does this because the pain throughout his or her body is inexplicable and uncontrollable. With self-mutilation, the child is inflicting a type of pain he or she can control and understand. Their self inflicted pain distracts them from chronic internal pain that they do not understand the source of. The child's cuts enable creation of a new pain in order to block out the old.

Re-examine your child's behavior and look for warning signs of this conduct due to sensory discomfort. These children often have itchy skin, psoriasis and eczema, gut pain, and headaches. Additionally, these children may experience some environmental discomfort as a result of certain sounds or light. One such sound would be equivalent to a foghorn being blown in a car with closed doors and windows. This would obviously be a very bothersome noise, but certain children experience this type of discomfort at far lower sound levels than that of a foghorn. Another example of sensory discomfort could come as a result of certain textures of food that can literally hurt the child's mouth. Other times, the food cannot be too mushy, too crunchy, or make a certain unpleasant sound.

Due to their over sensitivities, there are times when these kids will lock themselves in closets, build tents out of their blankets, or hide underneath tables. A behaviorist might attempt to pull the child out using a system of rewards and punishments. This method comes without fully understanding that the child is trying to self-medicate him or herself by reducing the amount of stimuli from light or sound. When the child is young, this behavior is quite appropriate. The reason the child is hiding in the dark is because he or she is trying to eliminate the sensory overload that is affecting them. If the bright lights or unpleasant sounds are hurting the child, his or her attempts to diminish this sensory overload are very

natural, and most often the only way the child knows how to reduce these stimuli. My advice to parents is to view this behavior as a step in the right direction in indicating the source of the problem.

You might find some Autistic children in your community walking around wearing large headphones or helmets to help block out noise. The problem with overly relying on such things as helmets and ear phones is that they can handicap children further because they do little to help children overcome their hyper sensitivities. Rather than overly relying on such crutches, helmets and earphones should be used as stepping stones, not long term solutions (on the other hand, helmet use for head banging is necessary for protection and is not a crutch). In order to prevent the reliance of helmets and ear phones into adulthood, time should be spent learning de-sensitizing techniques.

Gut Sensitivity Issues

The gut as a whole is tremendously sensitive and is responsible for many of the reactions in an autistic and ADHD-affected child. I personally believe, as highlighted in my *"Recovering Autism, ADHAD, and Special Needs"* video, that the gut affects the brain more than the brain affects the gut. Some think the gut holds as much ability as a second brain would. We have all heard of expressions such as "trust your gut," because the gut responds to nearly everything, including decision making; if only we could listen to the gut more often. Dr. Joseph Mercola, D.O., a graduate of Chicago College with a degree in Osteopathy, says that, "There are 100 trillion cells in your body," He

goes on to state that "the rest are bacteria, fungi, viruses and other microorganisms, i.e., your microflora…[and] researchers show they play [a] crucial role in your health." (Mercola, 2012)

A large number of children with Autism have chronic gut ailments; a common condition is Gastroesophageal Reflux Disease, also known as GERD. Sometimes the persistent vomiting and colic starts in infancy and sometimes later in childhood. In any case, regardless of onset, a much deeper issue exists.

The first sign of a problem comes when children with conditions such as GERD continue to vomit 10 or more times per day, yet somehow the pediatricians will seem to not listen. When the infant vomits, they'll tell you 'it's only colic and colic is normal'. They'll tell you that your child is "spicy." They'll tell you to try a different food to see if the vomiting goes away, and often enough they'll blame you, the parent, for this condition. At the age of three or four, referrals are made to a gastroenterologist, who will undoubtedly agree to perform a biopsy. The doctor might see a damaged esophagus due to years of stomach acids backing up and harming the esophageal lining. In some cases, unless remedied, this condition has been correlated to esophageal cancer down the road. Young children are often prescribed antacids to stop the vomiting and the acid build-up. This is sometimes effective but is often an antithetical treatment. The problem in actuality is not too much acid, but rather not *enough* acid.

Concerning the gut, these children are in pain and vomiting, suffer from chronic diarrhea and/or constipation, and often refuse to eat new and different kinds of food. You will notice that these children appear to tense up a lot, and surely their intestines tense-up as well. What appears to be happening is that the intestines become restricted and tighten-up. Somehow, the intestines seem to actually knot-up. Since they have digestion problems, some fecal matter can become trapped somewhere in the large intestines during the digestive process. For several days, the only thing that gets around the blocked excrement is liquid matter, resulting in blistering diarrhea. Eventually, the feces will begin to make its way down the intestines, only to lodge once again and cause further constipation. This constipation can become so painful that a child will stick a finger up their rectum to relieve some pressure, and sometimes will smear the feces on a wall to remove the substance from their hands.

Behaviorists will be alarmed at how outrageous this behavior is when a child flings fecal matter from his or her hand as a result of the child not knowing how to relieve this internal pressure without any of basic sense of hygiene or self-control. Sadly, severely autistic children who are flinging their feces around because they didn't fully understand what it means to be sanitary and act properly would stop at nothing to relieve their pain. In this example, I am emphasizing these children are using their hands because of their *physical* pain and not because they have a mental defect.

Contributing to the problem outlined above is the fact that the regular diet does not get broken down in these children's guts in a proper fashion. Once again, the culprit can be found in products that contain hidden ingredients such as milk, gluten, or soy. Many such children get huge relief from gluten-free and dairy-free diets, known as "GFDF." It is amazing to realize that approximately 25 years ago almost no one had ever heard of a gluten-free diet, but today you can shop at any food store and find a whole section of gluten-free products. According to the website *The Prepared Pantry*, "Gluten is a substance made up of the proteins found in wheat flour that gives bread its structure, strength, and texture." (The Prepared pantry, 2012) Gluten is also the component of food that tends to be water-insoluble, as a result many people cannot properly digest it even when they could just a few years prior. Some believe that gluten intolerance is related in part to genetically modified foods, while others believe that wheat and grains have become too much of a staple in our diets and that people were not meant to survive on such large amount of wheat in the first place. Additionally, selectively grown wheat was used in farming as far back as the 1950s and 1960s, which led to the altered state of wheat that we find in foods today. These modern strains of wheat were grown for their large yield, not for their digestibility. Also, the Gliadin in wheat is equally hard to tolerate. So, just having a gluten free diet does not fully address wheat sensitivity.

About 50 years ago, the American diet consisted more of meats and vegetables than it did of breads and cereals, people ate less-processed foods. When people think of typical carbohydrates found in breads, pasta, and cereals, people tend to forget that it converts to sugar in the body. The pancreas, which produces juices that help break down food, develops a hyper sensitivity to sugar from over eating of carbohydrates and leads to diseases such as diabetes, metabolic disorder, and pancreatitis. A question is then raised about the inordinate increase of diabetes today as well, especially amongst children.

Candida Infections

Getting back to autistic children, their abdomen always seems to be in pain. When these children are not having bouts of vomiting, diarrhea, or constipation, their guts are bloated and distended, sometimes after only just a few bites of food. They can whine that they are hungry, but when you serve them their meals they only take a few bites before announcing that they could not possibly eat anymore. They are *not* doing this to intentionally misbehave. Instead, they are doing this because of a physical problem. In this example, the problem might be an undiagnosed systemic internal infection, commonly known as Candida, a yeast-like, parasitic fungus.

Many special needs children are seemingly perpetually ill with one condition or another throughout infancy and childhood. They get ear infections, sore throats, eye infections, stomach viruses, croup, and everything else that goes around in pre-schools and elementary schools. They are prescribed antibiotics such as Ampicillin, Amoxicillin, Vibramycin, and Erythromycin (and anything else ending in "cin" or "cillin") over and over again to stop infection. The job of the antibiotics is to beat the infection and stop the bad bacteria. The antibiotics – unable to discriminate between bad bacteria and good bacteria –

kill the natural and beneficial bacteria in the gut as well. If a child takes a couple of rounds of antibiotics, an unintended side effect would be a large portion of the good bacteria from the gut can be killed. As a result, yeast, which normally exists in the lower part of the gut, now uninhibited by the good gut bacteria, will begin to overrun its growth through the formation of fungus spores, proliferating to different areas of the body where it does not belong. Eventually, this yeast will release toxic secretions throughout the body.

Yeast normally lives in the lower intestine, eating the protective mucosal layer that lines the sides. They live like a hungry army of Pacmen on the intestinal wall. This layer of mucous exists to protect the body from toxins and chemicals that could be potentially harmful. When the yeast depletes the lining, the yeast grows uncontrollably and can eventually make its way to the blood, lodging itself in the colon, clogging up the sinuses, the ears, and other orifices.

There are many symptoms of an active yeast infection. These symptoms include, but are not limited to: headaches, mood swings, stomach aches, gassiness and bloating, perpetual ear infections, eye infections, vaginal yeast infections, repeated urinary tract infections, cold hands and feet, constant exhaustion even after a full night's sleep, Thrush, Fibromyalgia, Chronic Fatigue Syndrome, different types of Arthritis, Depression, forgetfulness and a wide array of other symptoms. Men can also get yeast infections. It is interesting to note that men get just as many yeast infections as women, but do not recognize the condition as what it is.

There is a quick and simple home Candida test you can take to see if you or anyone in your family has a yeast infection. To do this, before doing anything else, especially brushing the teeth, spit into a clear glass of water first thing in the morning and check it every 15-20 minutes, monitoring the formation of the saliva in the water. If "leg-like" formations or spider webs pointing down toward the bottom of the glass are created by the saliva, or if the water is particularly cloudy and has specks in it, then you are likely to have Candida overgrowth. If, however, the water is relatively clear, then you might not have yeast overgrowth. Not having an overgrowth of yeast yields saliva that lays on the surface of the water, which forms bubbles-- and are without these spider web-like "legs" dangling down through the water towards the bottom of the glass. When attempting to cure yourself of a yeast overgrowth, it is a good idea to use the spit test at the beginning of your treatment plan and then try it again when you think you have accomplished your goal in order to monitor your progress. If the spit test has failed, it may be time to choose a different treatment option.

Other signs of a yeast infection are having "thrush" in the mouth, often seen as whitish patches in the mouth and throat. By looking at the tongue and the mouth, you will see that it is creamy and pasty. 'Thrush' is simply another name for a common type of yeast infection in the mouth and throat arising from the presence of Candida. Many babies have thrush nowadays, and to treat it doctors simply write a prescription for a mouth rinse that overcomes the yeast/thrush in the mouth.

However, this treatment does nothing to get to the root problem of the yeast, which lies in the gut. Only using the mouth rinse does a disservice to the child or baby much the same way in which a gynecologist prescribing an anti-fungal cream (such as Nystatin) to stop itchiness and bacteria imbalance in the vagina does a disservice to the woman if the root cause of the imbalance is not addressed. It is not enough to remove yeast that you can see on the outside without curing what is happening on the inside.

Many internal yeast infections such as Candida will not go away on their own. I cannot begin to describe to you how many health professionals and owners of health food stores are out there telling people that if they simply change their diet and stop eating carbohydrates and sweets the yeast infections will go away. This is not true. The yeast infection will slow down and not grow as quickly, but it's not likely that a yeast infection already in existence will suddenly disappear. As I said earlier, there are many products on the market that will help add Probiotics, or healthy bacteria, into the gut in order to kill off the yeast. There are several prescription medications that will kill a yeast infection at an accelerated pace and I am in favor of them, provided that you do not have a weakened liver. Using oral Nystatin, oral Diflucan, and others that may be prescribed by your doctor is similar to using a popular dieting quick-start program. I believe that starting with an oral prescription and ending with a natural remedy in conjunction with a change in diet will cover all angles.

Hearing Sensitivity

There is a medical condition by the name of "Hyperacusis." "Hyper-" is a prefix meaning "excessive," and "-acusis" relates to "the sense of hearing." When one has Hyperacusis, he or she has problems tolerating sounds that are moderate to loud. For instance, the noise of a vacuum cleaner, the sounds of someone breathing next to you, and rustling of papers can cause pain. Even writing with a pencil can be too loud or chillingly grating for some children, whereas writing with a pen is fine. These are sounds other people might not notice, whereas for these children those sounds are painful. According to the Euro Tinnitus Association, "the origin of Hyperacusis is in the central auditory nervous system, rather than in the ear (the cochlea)" (Euro Tinnitus Association, 2012). The association goes on to say that Hyperacusis "is more common in children with disorders such as: central auditory processing disorders, learning disabilities, attention deficit disorder (ADD), head injury, a history of chronic middle ear infections with conductive hearing loss, Autism, and autistic-like behaviors." I personally would add Dyslexia to that list.

While I am aware that some autistic children are so sensitive to sound that the only way the family can take him or her out of the house is with a cumbersome acoustic-blocking headphone set. It has bothered me that in the cases I observed, I have never seen the child get better from headphone use. The child never gets a chance to normalize to outside sounds; they remain overly sensitized year after year. That is not to say that they can't get better, I just have not witnessed them

getting better. According to James W. Hall III, Ph. D., a professor of hearing and speech sciences at Vanderbilt University, "People with Hyperacusis should be advised to avoid silence. The person's natural tendency is to seek out quiet. Some wear earplugs almost constantly to avoid as much exposure to sound as possible. This strategy is, in fact, counterproductive, because it is likely to prompt the central nervous system to increase gain even further. Hearing protection should be considered only when there is the likelihood of exposure to high-intensity sounds that could potentially cause noise-induced hearing loss or during extended periods of bothersome noise (e.g., riding in an airplane or a car)." Dr. Hall also states, "People with Hyperacusis typically have normal hearing, whereas loudness recruitment is associated with sensory hearing loss. A better term for loudness recruitment is "abnormal growth of loudness. People with Hyperacusis also have an abnormal growth of loudness, but it is a very different pattern from that seen with the typical person with cochlear (inner ear) pathology."

The takeaway here is that some lower sounds bother some of the patients some of the time; it is inconsistent. Whereas a vacuum cleaner might outrage an autistic child one day, the sound of the loud drum might not the next day. The sound of someone whispering or breathing might alarm an autistic child at lunch, but he or she might not be bothered by the sound of whistling wind in the next moment. Another example is when your child suddenly refuses to do his homework one day whereas yesterday he was fine. Yesterday he used a pen, today a pencil.

Something so simple can radically alter his disposition. He is not communicating the fact that the sound of the pencil is what is irritating him so greatly. Again, in Autistics, Hyperacusis is inconsistent and illogical.

Vision and Sight Sensitivity

Vision and sight issues are another major concern for autistic children. For example, many toddlers and children with Autism walk on their toes rather than putting the entire bottom of their foot down on the ground. Optemelogical therapists and physical therapists might say that these children have difficulty knowing where they are in space. Some of these kids tend to view the world in a two-dimensional, rather than a three-dimensional manner. Because of their trouble with spatial relationships, each step is labored. They have a regulation problem with their "Proprioception." The website MedicineNet.com states that Proprioception is "the ability to sense stimuli arising within the body. Even if you are blindfolded, you know through Proprioception if your arm is above your head or hanging by your side. The word 'Proprioception' was coined in 1906 by the English neurophysiologist Charles Sherrington who received the Nobel Prize for Physiology or Medicine in 1932 for research on the function of the neuron and study of reflex action" (MedicineNet.com, 2012).

Another aspect of vision impairment is when the two eyes don't track together adequately and can effect how the feet are moving in space. The left and right feet aren't really walking forward in tandem, but they are moving "left, right, left, right," separately and out of rhythm rather than "forward, forward." I cannot tell you how many times I have seen autistic children crash when trying to enter a doorway or fall off a stable chair while not moving.

Some eye doctors would say that people with ASD often have adequate focal vision, but very poorly developed ambient vision. I would take it even further and identify it as a problem of the left and right eyes not tracking together coupled with a distortion of Proprioception, which can account for a child reacting as if they lost their footing on a ship, feeling dizziness.

Some autistic children can see at great distances with enormous detail, like an eagle above a thick forest being able to zoom in on a tiny mouse. A particular autistic child might have a tantrum upon entering a room, for example, if a tiny gum wrapper were 30 feet away on the floor, because the item was not in its proper place. Their whole system can be thrown off and no one else would notice the tiny wrapper and know why the child is crying.

Many children also have extreme sensitivity to bright lights - even sunshine - that causes them great pain. With regards to sunshine or light sensitivity, it can be highly illogical. The child could be out playing in the sun all day but will panic if a slight amount of sun comes through the windows.

One of the most uncomfortable types of bright light is typically found in schoolrooms in the form of fluorescent lighting. The fluorescent green tint in these lights can feel painful to the children. At the same time these types of lights emit low levels of electro-magnetic radiation. This particular kind of lighting can hurt their eyes and give them headaches. When children are too young, they cannot convey this to you. Often, when they run and hide in the closet, they do so to reduce the intensity of the bright lights. To make matters worse, they cannot help but to focus on the buzzing sound the fluorescent lights make. All types of fluorescent bulbs contain some mercury and emit low levels of radiation. Caution should be taken in the home to not break them and have the family exposed to the mercury. If one breaks at a school, the school is supposed to call in a HAZMAT team to properly remove the pieces and emissions, which rarely is the case.

Other children are overly bothered by the light on smoke and other alarms. I once worked with a child who became greatly distressed from the tiny green light on a smoke alarm. While that child might have been crying, begging not to enter the room, you would have to be a private eye with keen detective skills to discover what the issue actually was.

Vision Impairment Issues

We humans have binocular vision, focusing by using both eyes together. Many special needs children (and even average but struggling students) have an eye that drifts, which in turn causes objects to appear as if they were moving even when they are not. As a result of this misalignment, to further simplify it, the left eye and the right eye do not properly track objects together with one another. When children stare off into space with seemingly no eye contact or communication, they can be doing so because their eyes might not be working properly in conjunction with one another, causing a superimposition of images. It is as if these children were in a film where colors and shapes were constantly shifting like a kaleidoscope. This visual movement is fascinating to them. This perceived motion of objects causes children to gaze in awe and enjoyment of the movement.

Sadly, doctors who go to assess what's wrong with a child (sometimes only in a few brief moments) observe the child staring into space and immediately prescribe all sorts of medications for this behavior. However, to prescribe a pill for what is really a vision problem not a behavior problem shows a complete lack of understanding. The child is simply fascinated by the ever changing shapes, colors, and motions they are seeing. Such children absolutely do not need to be prescribed anti-psychotic drugs; they are not experiencing a break from reality. For a medical professional, having a lack of understanding of the root cause of such conditions as this eye misalignment can cause serious harm. It does not take rocket science to figure out that such children with Autism or other special needs may not be seeing properly, simply by observing the children so affected. Even many eye doctors are not testing the eyes entirely. They prescribe glasses test and for near- and far-sightedness, but, sadly, not test how the two eyes work together.

A simple way to figure out whether your child's eyes track together, or if they are not binocular, is to observe your child reading or writing while he or she sitting at a desk or table. If your child is right handed, what you might find is that the left arm is extended out straight on the desk or table while his or her head is lying in the crux of the arm. It appears as if the child is tired and unmotivated. However, what the child is actually doing is blocking the vision of his or her left eye, and, as a result, he or she is actually reading or writing with the use of only the right eye. When a child sees only through the right eye, the double vision and superimposition stops. If the child does not compensate by leaning over when the eyes are not properly tracking together, the words will appear to move off the page and sometimes even as far as traveling onto a wall, especially at the end of the line.

A child who experiences this will generally dislike reading and writing, and often will be labeled as a special needs student or learning disabled. It is so sad to see that, in my more than 20 years of practice, the majority of special needs and struggling students have this issue. Please understand that it is the child's eyes - not the brain - most of the time. Where I reside, it took me 10 years to find four eye doctors in the entire state familiar with vision training. Often, as I found one doctor, another one was no longer taking new patients. A new office would open but an old doctor would retire. If you are noticing this condition in your child – by observing the child slouching over with his or her head cocked in his or her arm and the child's eyes drifting -- you can contact the Optometric Center of New York.[v] Tell them where you live and ask them which eye doctors are knowledgeable about vision training in your neighborhood. They should be able to give you a referral. The place they send you is akin to a gym for the eyes, only instead of exercise equipment they will use toys, gadgets, and film in order to help the child gain control of their vision. Sessions usually take place once a week for approximately 35 weeks at eye doctor offices or vision training facilities. See Chapter 7 for more information about vision training exercises.

In addition to this vision training, there are several simple computerized eye exercise programs that have come about recently. One of them is titled *Eye Can Learn* and has a variety of cartoon images and tracking exercises that your child can follow along with.[vi]

Sometimes special needs children do not want to play games or sports and it is assumed to be a behavioral problem when in actuality the child is having a vision problem, like when such a child sees two balls coming at them rather than one because of their double vision issues.

Parents often make comments that their children will read magazines such as *Sports Illustrated* and other publications without any problem. However, the minute their child has to read a required book for school, he or she will refuse, causing the parent to become judgmental, and making the child object to any reading whatsoever. This is no joke, and certainly no coincidence. There is unquestionably a much bigger issue at play. What actually happens is that when the child's eyes are not perfectly balanced reading a whole page in a book is difficult, but magazines are written in narrow columns, which are more easily tracked and read by children.

Another similar condition occurs when children constantly lose their place when reading. This forces children to read and reread the same sentences over and over again until they can fully understand the meaning of a passage. These children are also susceptible to a certain type of eyestrain, often leading to a slight headache. Problems such as those listed above rarely occur when print is laid out in narrow columns. By arranging words on the school book page in a similar manner to that which is commonly seen in magazines and newspaper pages, the issue of having difficulty in tracking from left to right is removed since the columns are narrower than typical books. For this reason, I believe that *all books* – schoolbooks, fiction and nonfiction alike, etc. – should be printed with pages containing narrow columns. It is not only better for school-aged children, but it can also benefit senior citizens, those who wear glasses and anybody in between who may need help focusing. With so many books now presently available for the iPad, Kindle, and other digital formats, it has in recent times become much easier to rearrange pages of books into columns, regardless of their original format. Thankfully, with a simple click, these new digital formats enable the reader to convert text to multiple columns.

Of all children listed as learning disabled in resource rooms or special education classrooms, up to 80 percent in my opinion struggle with reading, possibly as a result of this very common vision problem. Despite this large percentage, it is amazing to me that most eye care professionals have never worked with or heard about it. Many of these children, who struggle with reading year after year, can, with simple eye exercises, can then learn to read with ease.

As with other parts of this book, my attitude is this: If you are not sure whether or not your child has this issue, it would be worthwhile to learn about these exercises and try them. By doing so, you can decide whether to take your child to an eye doctor who is familiar with vision training or to use alternative methods instead.

Some vision training centers rely on a trampoline, a projector flashing words quickly across a screen, a metronome or 3D eyeglasses with red/blue patches, all of which are arranged for exercising and moving the left eye in sync the right eye. When correctly performed, these exercises can turn out to be a lot of fun for children to participate in. My professional experience has shown that some children require around 30 visits, some require only 12 visits, while others require around 40 visits. It is important to remind yourself that each child is different.

I must admit how diligent I was for many years in my academic sessions in making referrals to eye doctors who were adept in vision training. After finding local eye doctors who could perform vision training, I was asked to work with the children in my sessions but only make referrals if a child did not improve. Various materials were given to me in support (in fact, around that time a few computerized lessons came out). Presently, some insurance companies will pay for the vision training under the "eye care" portion with the doctor, and most will certainly pay for the initial (expensive) eye examination.

Developmental Issues

One of the problems with Autism is that the babies and children do not pass through the normal typical milestones of childhood development.

Oral development would be the first milestone, because infants learn about his or her world by putting everything in their mouth. Eventually a normal baby reaches a point where they no longer put things in their mouth, but this often does not happen with autistic children. Such children will continue to put things in his or her mouth, sometimes through the ages of 7 and 8, or indefinitely.

As normal infants develop, their experience of their world centers around eating and defecating, but for many autistic kids, this can be an indefinite time period as they seem to perpetually have problems with diarrhea, constipation, and issues with the toilet. They have trouble regulating and anticipating such as "how long will it be before I go to the bathroom?" Some autistic children play with their feces into all the way into adulthood.

I propose to identify such further developmental milestones such as a "shoelace stage," a "bike and ball stage," and a "teamwork communication stage."

The "shoelace stage", where a young child learns to tie their shoes, seems to last from approximately the ages of three and four up to the ages of five and six for normal children; with autistic kids, the problem can last indefinitely as well. There is a general clumsiness of the fingers and trouble sequencing what to do first, second, and last. Getting dressed in the morning for a 10-year-old who cannot tie his or her own shoes and requires assistance is also very difficult. Thankfully, many sneakers now have Velcro fasteners.

The "bike and ball stage", where a young child learns to ride a bike and to throw or catch a ball, for average children by the ages of seven and eight when they learn to ride a "big person" bike; in an autistic child, this stage can last up to 10 and 12, possibly even indefinitely. Many of these children will never be able to ride a bike. Having to remind your 12-year-old who might be able to ride a bike but doesn't remember to go to the bathroom is annoying to a caregiver. The parent is often thinking "How can this be happening to me."

My last stage is one of the most important stages, the "teamwork communication" stage. For autistic kids to learn to truly speak – not in a robotic fashion or in echolalia – the child has to reach a developmental stage at which a real and "normal" conversation can take place, one where you say something and the autistic child can communicate something back, and there's a real give and take. This point of development is a major component of "recovery."

Here is an illustration of a problem. Let's say your 7-year-old child is able to read and write, come home, and do homework, but will still pick up a penny from the floor and put it in his or her mouth. With "regular" kids, you have to watch them like a hawk when the baby is in the oral phase. But here, you have an older child you have to watch to make sure he or she does not swallow foreign items such as the penny.

The bottom line issue is that these kids do not pass through normal childhood developmental stage nor through the ones I just mentioned earlier as well. Oddly enough, all of a sudden, the child oftentimes will pass through all the stages as if in one day; you never know when that will happen. But, bear in mind that Autism is not something that is just simply outgrown; especially when a child is left to his or her own accord. Just because a doctor or other people may say that the child will outgrow their developmental issues, just waiting and choosing to do nothing will surely fail. Parents often hope to see incremental improvements over time; the fact of the matter is often little to no improvement is seen for long stretches and then suddenly many happen all at once. If you are a parent wondering if your child will get better or not, don't give up too soon. When you least expect it improvements will occur.

A more serious issue is that Autistic children often wander away from home, school, playgrounds, school buses, shopping centers, and elsewhere. It is an ongoing issue of serious consequences. I wish this were not the case. Assume it will happen sooner or later so that you will prepare a plan for dealing with this. It is a tragic story too often heard where a child is either lost and/or dies in the woods or is found drowned in some well, pond, or backyard swimming pool. Autistic children seem to naturally seek out bodies of water and wind up falling into them. All parents should put child-proof locks on doors that are out of their reach. Parents should make a list of bodies of water that their child has previously frequented such as little natural ponds, artificial goldfish ponds, and streams behind a friend's house. There are now a variety of companies that have created tracking devices that sound an alarm when your autistic child goes missing.

Another serious problem is confusion that arises when public authority figures are dealing with Autistic children. There are a few companies that have committed themselves to train policemen, fire departments, and rescue squads to engage with special needs children – but there are surely not enough of these because hundreds of times a year there are reports of a police officer telling a youth to put their hands up, and the autistic youth (who did not go through the "teamwork communication stage") are not able to follow directions or respond accordingly and they can easily wind up dead.

One particular sad case I recall is that a mother told her son to walk directly home after taking a pill. When a police officer thought he appeared agitated, he ordered the child to stop, and the child said, "No my mother ordered me to come home after taking this pill." The policeman thought the child was defying him, therefore potentially dangerous, and eventually he wound up shooting the child. He did not realize the child was Autistic, making this issue more of a tragedy. Regardless which tracking device, agency, or school program that you subscribe to, try to make it a point to let your trusted neighbors know in advance that if they see your child alone, to kindly let you know.

Other Issues with Autism

Something important to pay attention to while attempting to understand your child is to notice how he or she responds to directional commands. Directional instructions are how he or she responds to instructional-type commands. For example, tell the child to put the toy *next to* the bike, to put the stuffed animal *inside* the cubby, or to put the slippers *under* the table. Relative direction words such as above, behind, over, and under are usually difficult concepts for children at risk for ADHD and Dyslexia as well.

It is important for you to play games with your preschooler in which you emphasize command words. Bake with your child so that he or she may learn the importance of sequencing, that is, what comes first, second, and last. Teach the child to organize by sorting items based on colors, shapes, and sizes. By observing specific areas of your child's life and by putting the extra effort in when your child is in preschool, your unfocused and somewhat hyperactive child might just jump into their ABC's.

Speech delays should be another cause for an immediate red flag. The earlier speech therapy begins, the better the outcome. While some doctors recommend a wait-and-see approach, I think it is far better to get speech therapy early than miss the opportunity. Attending a few sessions does no harm, even if your child does not need to continue. Delaying necessary speech therapy can have serious long-term consequences.

Another issue that frequently arises in special needs children is the inability to fall and stay asleep, which may turn into quite a problem both during the day and most notably at night. Because of their hypersensitivity, a child will not be able to sleep due to a change in temperature or barometric pressure, food digestion, fear of lights or shadows, or for unknown reasons. Some parents have turned to the use of Melatonin to assist with this issue, which is much better than the overuse of sleeping pills. After checking with your family doctor, you might be amazed that Melatonin is found in the vitamin section of your local pharmacy or food store. There are essential oils and herbal teas that have helped as well. Parents should do their own research on possible remedies.

Another symptom to be on the lookout for when the child is an infant or toddler is having repeated infections, particularly of the ear. As a common treatment, antibiotics are routinely prescribed. However, these antibiotics can alter the gut flora, the healthy bacteria that live in the gut. As previously stated, antibiotics kill the infection, but as a side effect they also kill the healthy bacteria. You can look for and experiment with multiple ways to prevent or reduce ear infections. Health food stores sell garlic oil made for children's ears. Additionally, a child might benefit from taking probiotics, (e.g., acidophilus), the healthy gut bacteria that antibiotics can harm. It is better to use multi-strain probiotics because each strain works differently in the body and all are necessary for optimum digestive health. Parents will benefit with their use as well. The very best probiotic sources can be found in liquid form and are refrigerated.

By Observing Your Child's Symptoms, We Can Generate Recovery

Just like many parents already know that when an infant or toddler pulls on an ear, its time to take a closer look to see whether the child has an ear infection, the messages that these children are trying to tell us are not to be take for granted. You'll find some children screaming when food is being prepared or it is time to eat. The slightest thing, like the smell of an

open can of tuna can have some of these kids throwing things, banging their heads, or other similar behaviors. The idea is to remove these triggers as they grow up. By removing each level of illness, pain, and discomfort, we then have simply a child, who is ready willing and able to learn. How can we teach a child who is banging his head in pain that 1+1=2 when he is suffering? That would be equivalent to trying to train a dog how to walk properly on a leash when two of his legs are broken.

These activities are actually forms of self-medicating. The fort reduces the light that might be overloading the child's system. The sound of the television may be like an explosion, therefore the fort or closet muffles the noise.

If you put him in a sports program, imagine how the combined effects of the bouncing basketball, the view, echoing roar of the crowd, and florescent lights might seem to him: like "bombs bursting in air".

When you see her pulling off her shirt, the fabric is itchy to her, the tag digging into the skin. It's like sandpaper to her skin. He may need to wear the same colors every day and that is fine for now. Also, perfumes, soaps, cleansers, irritate him beyond imagination.

Certain textures in foods or colors can entirely disrupt her system. Any food dye with a number (i.e., red #5, blue #1, etc.) in such snacks as grape soda and cherry-flavored candy are made of tar and petroleum, which damage the functional health of the child. These poisons are used because they are cheaper than fresh fruits.

He may have food sensitivities to milk, soy proteins, wheat, gluten, and so on. Sometimes even vitamins are not properly digested or absorbed. Many of these children have skin problems such as rashes and eczema.

Keep in mind that often it can be the gut interfering with the brain, rather than the brain interfering with the child. One thing to consider is that the adjuvants within a vaccine that are put there to hyper stimulate the child's immune system so that it reacts to the virus proteins, also inadvertently cause immunological hyper sensitivity to other previously innocuous proteins (peanuts, milk, wheat, etc.) that may enter the body, often times resulting in anaphylactic shock.

Let's look at some practical solutions for your child regardless of the diagnosis:

1. If your child is not verbal, begin speech therapy IMMEDIATELY.

This does not have to necessarily be Applied Behavioral Analysis (ABA) because there are many other effective methods out there.

2. If she/ he falls a lot or is clumsy, you must begin to employ physical therapy IMMEDIATELY.

3. If she/he cannot draw or paint, begin occupational and/or art therapy IMMEDIATELY.

4. Another avenue for desensitizing is Sensory Integration Therapy (SIT).

Try to get these services through your insurance, local school district, university, hospital, or private therapy. Do whatever it takes! If possible, barter services if you have to, i.e., hair-cutting, house-cleaning, healthy meals on wheels, piano lessons, etc.

Time is of the essence, as I expressed previously. This because a window of opportunity exists -- approximately between the ages of birth and approximately nine or ten -- when the brain is still flexible and amenable to learning, and can regenerate, opening new, fertile pathways to cognitive and social skills. The latest research shows that the brain is plastic and can be re-mapped; reassigning into other areas, which effectively reprograms the child's capabilities. So the good news is by starting early you buy more time for your child with each intervention. And this window of opportunity can be extended even to the age of eleven, twelve or higher!

Fortunately, the sooner these services are in place, the better the child will get regardless of their official diagnoses. I have seen many young people with these disorders eventually go on to live healthy independent lives. On the other hand I know children who have ended up in group homes or worse due to a lack of services, denial, and a lack of community support.

In summation, all children with one or all of these diagnoses share certain traits: their sense of smell, sight, touch, and hearing is acutely heightened. If your child is always alone, perpetually grabbing blankets and hiding under the table, building forts, or hiding in the closet, she/he is giving you vital information. Watching out for these symptoms is how you can learn what is needed to essentially cure your child. Keep in mind that it is the preponderance of symptoms that interfere with normal functioning, not any one particular behavior, that is the basis for a diagnosis.

To elaborate the point that it is not just particular behaviors, I have had some clients insist that their children were Autistic because they exhibited some strange behaviors, but as I worked with their children I found no Autism whatsoever. The mothers would say "the child lines up his toys, was speech delayed, had a narrow focus of interests", concluding that their child was indeed Autistic. While it was acknowledged that the child had some quirky behaviors, the reason they were not Autistic was because the child was easily able to change or transition their actions, such as put their toys away when asked, go to one place to another without disruption, shift from one activity to another with ease, and so on. Thus, the child was fully functioning, despite having the occasional odd behavior.

All in all, Autism is not one single illness, but a battery of multiple illnesses. The truth is that regardless of the diagnosis, as a parent you should do your best to deal with a WHOLE child, from soup to nuts; from their head to their toes.

One day as I was driving on an entrance ramp to a local highway, I saw a deer with an arched back, and it was flailing up and down in place while throwing its head to the left and to the right. It appeared like a cartoon. I was wondering if the deer had rabies. It then dawned on me that just a moment ago, the car in front of me had stopped short; it must have hit the deer. It was not just that the deer was wildly prancing, but that it was acting bizarre and swaggering because it was in severe physical *pain*. As a parent of a severely autistic child, you may observe your child jumping up and down and having bizarre erratic behavior that is not different from that of this erratic deer. And so, "deer" parents, you too can get your little ones out of physical pain, one layer at a time.

Without question you have been dealt a very difficult hand. But I believe that a parent in such a position as yours can develop what it takes to solve the puzzle. As a parent you should accept your limitations and forgive yourself for having them. For example you may come to the conclusion that you will not be able to home school your special needs child and will need to hire a special needs tutor. You need a break and let the preschool in your district provide services. Also, you and the rest of the family will need respite care and downtime. It is estimated that it takes over 3 million dollars to raise one Autistic child, so you are entitled to a break.

In prior times mothers helped each other out if they had to go on an appointment; one of the other mothers on the block would watch your children and vice versa. If there ever were a time in which a child got sick from a vaccine or doctor's appointment, the other mothers would quickly spread the news and make sure that no one would go there again. In those days, generally there was a working father, a stay-at-home mother with a house, televisions, and two cars.   But today, the father works full time, the mother works full time, the children are in day care and are supervised by the lowest paid employee of all professions. The children are growing-up angry; we now have to worry about guns in schools and everyone is exhausted. Yet still with both parents working, we cannot afford the house, the cars, and even vacations.

No one got liberated like they thought they would; they got more enslaved. Most of all, when a child has seizures, becomes ill, becomes autistic, or dies from a vaccine, women barely even have the time to talk to each other about what happened; they are completely cut off from each other and in some ways, from their families. We have got this "too busy" type of world. To reiterate a constant theme in the book, at this point in time, one out of every five children is neurologically impaired; one out of every six children now has a developmental disability; another one out of six has learning disabilities. Though these numbers are high, all countries around the globe that are beginning to follow our vaccination schedule are having similar results. This child impairment is of epic proportions: one in 38 in South Korea, enormous numbers in Australia, the UK, and all the other countries that are going down the same rabbit hole.

This chapter includes issues that may appear unrelated but are in fact very interrelated. By studying these symptoms, and perhaps separating the layers, you can affect recovery, if not a "cure."

Chapter 3: ADHD, What is It Really?

Attention Deficit Hyperactivity Disorder (ADHD) is a common childhood developmental disorder that is difficult to diagnose and even harder to understand. This disorder negatively affects children's behavior. ADHD is characterized by either significant difficulties of inattention or hyperactivity and impulsiveness or a combination of the two.

Actually, it is not that they are specifically inattentive; rather they are overly attentive to every detail in the room around them, which distracts them greatly. For example, while you are trying to talk to them about something important, they are listening but also thinking about the wallpaper behind you, the color of your shoes, the dusts specks on the floor, all the while keeping their eyes on their computer.

Children with ADHD are often disruptive, restless, impulsive, and find it hard to focus, which impairs their ability to learn properly. Some ADHD children, adolescents, and adults have difficulties with social skills, such as social interaction and forming and maintaining friendships. Oftentimes, these children talk back to teachers, get suspended in school, leave their school work all over, etc. They are often the target of bullies, which means you must be diligent that they don't develop into bullies themselves.

ADHD is a phenomenal diagnosis; its numbers grew out of nowhere in the early 1990s; it exploded onto the scene. Rivaled only by the plethora of medications, there is Ritalin, Concerta, Adderall, Vyvanase (which is nothing but repackaged Dexadrine), and others that suddenly appeared in the 1990s and have been around ever since.

While doing research for this book, I came across a startling fact from the website *Bupa.co.uk*; they stated that as recent as April 2011, "around one in 25 boys" are diagnosed with ADHD (Bupa's Health Information Team, 2011). According to the website *USAToday. com*, a government survey says that one in ten kids has ADHD and it's a sizeable difference from just a few years ago (Mozes, 2011).

According to the Center for Disease Control (CDC), some data and statistics in the US have been reported saying that the percent of children with a reported ADHD diagnosis increased by 22% within the 4 years of 2003-2007. Rates of ADHD diagnosis increased in average of 3% a year from 1997-2006 and an average of 5.5% per year from 2003-2007. Boys being diagnosed with ADHD outnumber by far girls diagnosed with the same condition (Morbidity and Mortality Weekly Report, 2010).

Despite the percentages as reported by the CDC, it appears that as many as about 30% of public school children at any given time can be found lining up at the school nurse's office for medication.

Typically ADHD children do a lot of extreme fidgeting, such as rocking a foot back and forth, tapping their fingers while playing "paradiddles," nervously looking around, and have great difficulty making friends and keeping their peer relationships. They misplace things constantly, at times they may do their homework but forget to submit it, and tend to zone out when it comes to figuring out how much time is needed to complete tasks. In general, not only are these children highly distractible, but also they are very unorganized.

In some instances, children with ADHD start to become very literal about rules as they start to improve with age. For example, if you stop for a moment to go into a store and there is a sign there saying not to park here, the child panics about this. They can't adjust to the circumstance.

They also become master negotiators, weighing every little detail in an argument. For example, the child says to their parent, "If you are going to make me come to dinner before my video game is over, then you have to let me stay up an extra hour so I can finish my game." There are many "If, then statements" and every situation becomes a negotiation. In some instances this can work for you as a parent, rather then against you. It is always a great idea to structure their routine so that they do their homework first when they arrive from school. Otherwise the child will negotiate all night long and still not do their homework, saying he has to watch his favorite show first or practice first or finish a game first or make a phone call first and so on until it is too late.

People with ADHD have a tendency to have addictive personalities that can lead them into anti-social behaviors, including alcoholism, drug addiction, promiscuity, and gambling. In different forms of ADHD, there may be a pattern where the children constantly cry, whine, or show great mood swings at a young age.

Early ADHD Symptoms to Look for

Long before long-term problems set in, you might be able to catch signs of a major problem beginning at home in your toddler or preschooler before it becomes too late. There is not one particular symptom that indicates early childhood ADHD, but rather there are a group of behaviors that may be of concern. By identifying certain behaviors of your child, you may actually improve the situation before he or she will inevitably begin to struggle in school. By catching the symptoms early and exposing your child to some form of early intervention, you might even be able to remedy the situation.

For more specific instructions, here is an article that I authored for *Holistic Remedies News* regarding ADHD preschool symptoms:

ADHD Preschool Symptoms - Clues Most Parents Miss

ADHD can show up in the preschool years but the symptoms are often overlooked. Years ago the preschool teacher might have called the parents to explain that the child had displayed "Odd" behaviors or did not seem to fit in. Today, that call is extremely rare. Teachers are not so eager to inform the parents. For one thing the parent might blame the school and simply take their child to a different school. Another reason that they are reluctant to inform the parent is because some classes have a large number of children with issues. It seems as if it is fast becoming the "norm."

There is not one particular symptom that indicates early childhood ADHD but rather it is a group of behaviors that are of concern. By identifying certain behaviors you might actually improve the situation before your child struggles in elementary school. By catching the symptoms and exposing your child to some form of early intervention, you might be able to remedy the situation.

Here are some symptoms to watch for. Your daughter may be whining and screaming a lot, way more than other toddlers.

Difficulty sleeping is common (hers as well as yours). He or she may be behaving in a bossy manner. You call his or her name but get ignored. You ask your child to follow 2 or 3 simple instructions and they refuse to do what was asked. You might say, "Shut the TV and come to the table for lunch." After being ignored you go over and shut it yourself and begin to have a tense attitude. You do not like being ignored.

Understand that you are not being ignored but that your child might not be processing what you are saying. He or she might have an "Auditory Processing Disorder, or an "Auditory Glitch." You can check to see if this might be one part of the equation. Gently ask your child, "What did you hear me say?" If he or she attempts to repeat the instruction and can not-you may just have an answer. Imagine what might have occurred in a class with 15 kids in the room if your child can not repeat what was said in a one to one situation? One solution is to make sure that you have eye contact when requesting that the TV be turned off.

The bossiness can indicate that the child is not learning social cues. They do not know how to get others to want to cooperate and become too demanding. Demands have the opposite effect

of what your son or daughter is seeking. Other children can begin to be repelled. Gently teach this. Try using puppets to teach your child what works best when with other children.

The inability to fall asleep or stay asleep can turn into quite a problem for both day and night. Some parents have turned to the use of "Melatonin" to assist with this issue. After checking with your family doctor, you might be amazed that it is found in the vitamin section of your local pharmacy or food store.

Other areas to watch for are how he or she responds to direction type commands. Put your toy, "Next to," your bike. Put your stuffed animal, "Inside," your cubby. "Put your slippers "Under," the table. Words such as above, behind, over and under are usually difficult concepts for children at risk for ADHD.

Speech delays are a red flag. The earlier speech therapy begins, the better the outcome. Some doctors recommend a "Wait and see approach. I think it is far better to get speech therapy early, than miss the opportunity. No harm is done by getting some sessions. Delaying speech therapy if needed can have long-term consequences.

Another symptom to watch out for is a toddler that has repeating infections, particularly ear infections. Antibiotics are routinely used to stop infections but they can alter the "Gut Flora," or healthy bacteria in the gut. Antibiotics kill the infection but simultaneously kill the healthy bacteria. You can look for ways to prevent or reduce ear infections. Health food stores sell garlic oil made for children's ears. A child might benefit from taking acidophilus, the healthy bacteria that antibiotics can harm.

Play games with your preschooler emphasizing the command words. Bake with your child so that he or she learns the importance of sequencing; what comes first, second and last. Teach her or him to organize by sorting items into colors, shapes and sizes.

By observing these areas and putting in the extra effort when your child is in preschool, your unfocused somewhat hyperactive child might just jump into their ABC's.

ADHD Recovery Issues

The exact cause of ADHD is not known, but some claim there are genetic factors. Others claim that there are medical and environmental factors that are the primary underlying root cause. Regardless of origin, cases of ADHD are continually on the rise. This situation would not be true if ADHD was strictly a genetic disorder rather than a physical one.

On closer inspection, it can be discovered that the vast majority of children diagnosed with ADHD in actuality really have Candida / yeast infections. The symptoms of both conditions overlap nearly identically. Treating children for yeast infections alleviates most of their ADHD symptoms as well. Such children seem to have an inability to sit still, concentrate, or even remember things. They too tend to have medical problems such as itchy skin or recurring ear infections that seem unrelated, but can be overlooked symptoms of a systemic internal infection that indeed may be Candida and yeast.

Frequently, after vaccinations, children start to come down with reoccurring ear infections, possible strep throat, bronchitis, sinusitis, and even urinary tract infections. The typical treatment prescribed for these infections are antibiotics. While those help, they can also simultaneously damage a child, as they are not able to discriminate between good and bad bacteria. Every human has yeast in the lower part of the gut, as well as "good" bacterium that keeps the yeast in place. Once the healthy, normal bacteria get destroyed, yeast starts to proliferate and grows where it does not belong.

When finished, the yeast more or less overtakes the system. The symptoms of ADHD and a yeast infection gone amuck are nearly identical. A yeast-infected child or adult will have a hard time concentrating or sitting still. They have specific food cravings, trouble with their memory, and may be fatigued after a long night's sleep; they also tend to have athlete's foot, jock itch, fungal infections, or repeating urinary tract infections. Children and adults often tap their feet, sway, and always appear like they're ready to play the drums. Other telltale signs include cold hands or feet, gas, diarrhea, or bloating. They may tend to sound like a hypochondriac, when actually the yeast is causing discomfort. The yeast has traveled to different regions of the body.

Regarding the cold hands and feet, sometimes the affected are getting diagnosed with Reynaud's Disease, but more often than not, their hands and feet are cold from a reduction of proper circulation affected by Candida and yeast. According to the Mayo Clinic (2011), "Reynaud's Disease is a condition that causes some areas of your body – such as your fingers, toes, the tips of your nose and your ears – to feel numb and cool in response to cold temperatures or stress. In Reynaud's disease, smaller arteries that supply blood to your skin narrow, limiting blood circulation to affected areas. Women are more likely to have Reynaud's Disease. It's also more common in people who live in colder climates. Treatment of Reynaud's Disease depends on its severity and whether you have any other health conditions. For most people, Reynaud's Disease is more a nuisance than a disability". I have experienced meeting women who were diagnosed with Reynaud's that actually moved their families to southern climates as a part of their treatment. What's sad is that many of them could have recovered had they had the knowledge to kill-off their ongoing

yeast condition.

The circulation in the hands gets diminished and as such the hands get cold. Candida spreads throughout the whole body. Often times, your child will be diagnosed with having thrush, which is a fancy term for a yeast infection; it is in the mouth. Infants and babies tend to have a lot of rashes and red rashes as if they have been sitting in a burning diaper all day.

A common scenario with a yeast-infected child is that they tell the parents they are very hungry and almost starved. The meal is presented and the child might take a few bites and announce that they are full, only to return an hour later hungry again. Many parents will complain, "If only you had eaten an hour ago I wouldn't have to cook again," but it is not the child's fault. What happens is the yeast eats and expands first, and then defecates into the child. This makes him or her gassy and bloated. Their stomach distends and the child feels full right away. It can be seen then that ADHD is a physical illness and not a psychiatric disorder. Do not take offense because it is not your homemade cooking, not your decoration of the dinner table, it is just a reaction of a person with yeast and Candida overgrowth.

Following is an article I wrote about the connection between Candida and ADHD, originally published in the North Central edition *New Jersey Natural Awakenings Magazine* in August of 2010.

Alternative Treatments for ADHD

Many children today, far more than in previous generations, are diagnosed with Attention Deficit Disorder, ADD, or Attention Deficit Hyperactivity Disorder, ADHD. Much of the time, a pattern emerges. Not always, but frequently, the child has had a variety of ear infections, strep throat, sinus infections, particularly after receiving certain vaccinations.

The child may have had multiple antibiotics to treat the infections. Sometimes the antibiotics have been necessary to stop the invading bacteria. Unfortunately, antibiotics cannot discriminate between good and bad bacteria. As a result, an overgrowth of yeast, single-celled fungi, occurs. Even newborns, who've never taken antibiotics, can be born with thrush, a yeast infection exhibited in the baby's mouth, if the mother took antibiotics while pregnant. She may have unknowingly passed a yeast infection in utero.

Joseph Mercola, M.D., reminds us that our intestines are home to 60 trillion bacteria, "ten times the number of cells that live in [the] whole body." He says that sugar serves as "fertilizer" for the bad bacteria and yeast. About 80 percent of our immune system lives in our gastrointestinal tract, so it's important to optimize the ratio of the good bacteria to the bad bacteria. Everyone has yeast in the lower intestinal region; but when exposed to several rounds of antibiotics, the good bacteria is harmed and yeast overgrows, damaging the protective mucous lining of the intestines. With proliferation, yeast becomes an internal systemic problem.

For children, this may exhibit as sugar cravings for candy or carbohydrates. Yeasts demand what they need in order to multiply and grow stronger. A parent may be irritated that a child says he's hungry, only to watch the child take a few bites and walk away from the rest of the meal. An hour or two later, the child returns, hungry again. Though it is a frustrating situation, there may be something else at work. If it is yeast, the child ate little, but the yeast actually ate first. Then the yeast "defecated." At that point, the child may have felt full or gassy.

The scientific community has long investigated whether sugar produces hyperactivity in children. In the May 2010 issue of Clinical Pediatrics, Randi Hagerman, M.D., and Alice Falkenstein, M.Sc.W., published an interesting study in which they reported a clear relationship between ear infections and hyperactivity. In earlier research, the pair had noted "Ear infections and their effect on language development are a prominent topic in the pediatric literature. Hyperactivity has also been a hot item, of interest to not only pediatricians but also to parents, educators, daycare personnel and anyone who interacts with children. On the surface they seem to be two unrelated entities. But could there be a connection between these two conditions?" Subsequent studies have pointed to just such a connection.

The yeast-infected child will often display the same symptoms as the child with ADHD. These include, but are not limited to, poor concentration, inability to sit still, poor memory, jumping from place to place, not completing projects, homework, chores, and so on. Such children also tend to have cold hands or feet; suffer from stomachaches, mood swings, headaches, and itchy skin; and have dark circles under their eyes—just part of an endless list of problems. Because yeast travels from place to place, the child may complain of constipation on Monday only to suffer from diarrhea by Friday.

What can parents of such children do? Before seeking a prescription for ADHD, they would do well to have a medical practitioner advise how to reduce the yeast. According to Dr. Nikki Conte, a naturopath from Watchung New Jersey, nikkiconte-naturopath.com, "Systemic yeast infections can be treated through the use of herbs, homeopathy, supplements, and diet changes. It can be a bit challenging in kids as far as compliance," she says, but "Naturopaths can do a stool analysis to confirm yeast, Candida or issues such as parasites or other bacteria."

In his book *Help for the Hyperactive Child*, William G. Crook, M.D., encourages an elimination diet restricting sources of sugar. What was his advice? "For this, one removes the suspected foods from the diet for 5 to 10 days, until a convincing improvement in symptoms is seen. Then one returns the eliminated foods to the diet, one food each day, to see if symptoms return. Symptoms may be noticed within a few minutes, or they may not occur for several hours or until the next day."

While a stringent diet certainly helps reduce yeast overgrowth, a yeasty child may struggle to resolve symptoms fully through diet alone. The following tips have proven helpful in the reduction of systemic yeast in children and adults alike.

• Probiotics. These are good bacteria; the term means "for life." According to Medicine.net, most probiotics are bacteria similar to those naturally found in the gut, especially in those of breastfed infants (who have natural protection against many diseases). Most often, the bacteria come from two groups, Lactobacillus or Bifidobacterium. Acidophilus replaces some of the healthy bacteria. It is the live active culture found in some brands of yogurt. Choose yogurts with live and active cultures that are low in fat or nonfat without lots of extra sugar. Pay attention to the expiration date; live cultures diminish with time.

• Garlic is thought to have anti-fungal properties.

• Beneficial supplements such as Yeast Away and Yeast-Guard have a mixture of ingredients to combat yeast growth.

• Consult a holistic physician or naturopath. If she diagnoses your child with a yeast infection, she may prescribe oral Fluconazole or Nystatin, antifungal drugs.

• Become friends with a trusted local health food store manager, who could prove to be a source of good information on natural treatments for yeast infections.

If you see marked improvement in your child, he or she may not need other kinds of prescription medications. Children vary in their resolution of yeast. Be patient. If yeast is part of the problem, it can take from three months to more than a year to achieve solid results. There are also practical simple solutions that you, the parent, can take to encourage a healing home environment.

• Yeasty kids tend to suffer from allergies. They are hypersensitive to mold that forms in damp basements. Try a spray solution of water and vinegar on the basement wall and floors.

• For better sleep, reduce dust mites by wrapping the mattress or purchasing a dust mite protector, as long as it is placed entirely around the bed. Wrapping a mattress entails covering it with plastic from top to bottom including all sides, to make it airtight so that any dust mites will suffocate and die off. You can either purchase an airtight mattress protector, or visit a mattress store that typically delivers mattresses in plastic and then discards the plastic, and request that plastic.

• Clean and remove dust from air vents.

• Remove carpeting when there are wood floors.

• Reduce the numbers of stuffed animals displayed in your child's bedroom. Keep the ones not on display in airtight bags in a closet and rotate them every few weeks. The bag will stop the supply of oxygen to the dust mites.

In time, your child may become calmer and more focused when yeast and allergies have been addressed. He or she may even listen and follow instructions better. The best you can do for your child is combine your instincts with education so that he or she can live the healthiest, happiest possible life.

Shelley Tzorfas has been tutoring children with Dyslexia, ADD, and other learning challenges for more than twenty years. She holds an M.F.A. degree from Rutgers University and has studied education at Hunter College and NYU. She is a member of the International Dyslexia Society. Contact her at stzorfas@gmail.com or visit the website www.betterschoolresults.com

After the Candida treatments are completed, and any food allergies and food dye sensitivities are controlled, next you can follow through eye exercises. Structured activities and structured downtime are very helpful to get ADHD children to learn how to moderate their activities. Additionally, having them participate in sports and music activities helps them to redirect their unfocused energy, having their high energy work with them rather than against them.

Chapter 4: Understanding Dyslexia

Many people believe that they know what Dyslexia is; they think it is a problem in which letters are reversed or people somehow see backwards. The term was used in medical journals by James Hinshelwood M.A. M.D., in the 1890s and early-1900s; this man also authored *"Congenital Word-Blindness"* in 1917. In this book, Hinshelwood states that congenital word blindness is a subject that has gradually gained attention from medical professionals, especially from those engaged in educational work. In chapter two of the book *"The Right to Read,"* it states, "Hinshelwood concluded that the root of congenital word-blindness lay in children's brains because he had observed that dysfunctional reading symptoms found in adults with brain lesions were analogous to those of certain children with reading problems" (Hinshelwood, 1917).

It is interesting to note that James Hinshelwood was actually an eye doctor, an ophthalmologist. Hinshelwood speculated that there were brain lesions that caused some of the problems. It is because of his work that many people came to believe that dyslexics often see backwards or upside-down; most do not.

The International Dyslexia Association voted in 1994 on a new definition of Dyslexia and decided to make this their definition: Dyslexia is "neurologically-based, often familial, disorder which interferes with the acquisition and processing of language. Varying in degrees of severity, it is manifested by difficulties in receptive and expressive language, including phonological processing, in reading, writing, spelling, handwriting, and sometimes in arithmetic. Dyslexia is not a result of lack of motivation, sensory impairment, inadequate instructional or environmental opportunities, or other limiting conditions, but may occur together with these conditions. Although Dyslexia is life-long, individuals with Dyslexia frequently respond successfully to timely and appropriate intervention".

I personally am uncomfortable with this definition of Dyslexia because it makes Dyslexia seem as if it is merely an academic problem occurring during the school day, when it is actually a 24/7 problem. Dyslexia also has physical ramifications. For example, some dyslexics have difficulty attempting to ride on an escalator; they can get dizzy or tend to do a count off to be able to get on and

off this machine, often holding on to the handrails with both hands. Other children outgrew doing this behavior, but Dyslexics do not.

Before my own Dyslexia was diagnosed, I remember watching some mothers in the shopping mall holding babies in one arm, the stroller in the other arm, packages hung by their fingers, and toddlers hanging on to their jackets, gracefully descending the escalator. I remember wondering where they got their "talent" from. Years later, I discovered that these mothers were not talented, but that I was somewhat uncoordinated because of my Dyslexia when it came to some forms of motion. However, I was very athletic … these dyslexic tendencies were inconsistent with my ability to perform various sports skills (tennis, baseball, and archery). Another thing is that dyslexics can be terribly disorganized and have trouble remembering on a daily basis where they placed everyday objects. For example, running late and needing to find one's keys, and then rushing around looking for them and not processing the seeing of them when they are right in front of you. These people can also zone out when it comes to time; they think they have ample time to get somewhere or to complete something, but it takes longer than what they thought and it always amazes them.

As a dyslexic *myself*, I have coined a definition that seems to cover some of these misunderstandings and/or confusions. In my opinion, a more accurate description of Dyslexia is that it is a "processing of information problem, either in the visual, auditory, or kinesthetic mode".

Teachers often think that a child cannot be dyslexic if there are no reversals, but that is an incorrect and outdated statement. It can be a combination of all three modes or might show up by itself. When working with a dyslexic child, the best approach is to find the type – whether it be auditory, visual, or kinesthetic, and then use the child's strengths to reduce their weaknesses. The most important thing is to teach the child compensation methods. A child can have Dyslexia in writing, but not reading. Sometimes it can be in mathematics known as dyscalculia. It can show up in handwriting known as Dysgraphia or it can show up in the spoken word.

In my opinion, the most common form of Dyslexia is an auditory type. When there is a possibility of auditory Dyslexia, the sounds of the spoken words go into the ear and eardrum just fine; the ears work. But the child's processing of what you just said is the problem. It is as if there is a time delay, like when you are on a mountain and say something and then there is an echo following. You say something and there is an echo three times; the child will "hear" the third "echo." A simple example is let's say you give a child five verbal instructions such as, "Go to your room, put away your Lego blocks, get your yellow jacket, grab your blue notebook, and meet me downstairs." An hour later, the parent might go up to the child's room and find the child still playing with Lego blocks. The parent, now annoyed, will ask, "Why didn't you do what I told you to do?" but the child will say, "I did exactly what you said!" The child is telling the truth, they heard "go to your room" and "Legos." They did not

process the rest of the instructions; thus, upon hearing the word "Legos," they sat on the floor of their bedroom and began to play. A power struggle ensues because the parent is convinced that the child is always lying because the parent does not realize that the child has a processing problem. The parent needs someone who works with dyslexics to enlighten them.

Another example is when a parent asks a child to take care of the dog by feeding and walking it. The child might say, "You told me to feed him but you didn't say AND walk him." This is perplexing because in this case the parent would have expected the child to know that in order to take care of the dog, they would have to both feed AND walk the dog.

When a child has auditory Dyslexia, they are often not able to take notes while a teacher is speaking in a classroom setting. Either they can sit and listen OR they can take notes. They have the double load of having to process *understanding* the words and at the same time *how* to write the words to the paper. For example, when shifting from script to print lettering there is normally a moment of hesitation during the transition. Dyslexics tend to have a longer period of transitioning and are forced to be overly conscious of what they are writing (much the same way a normal person would feel the shaky transition when trying to use their less dominant hand). Writing, spelling, and typing may be automatic to you, but it is *not* automatic to a dyslexic. They require the utmost of concentration in order to simply write. While they are concentrating on the writing, they cannot concentrate on the listening; it is an *either / or* situation. Please note that whether your child has auditory Dyslexia or auditory processing disorder, he or she is entitled to receive in school via special needs planning someone else's notes as a backup, either the teacher's or another student's.

Patterns of speech can show that the child has Dyslexia as well. An example of this can be found when you ask a child to tell the story of the Wizard of Oz and it goes something like this:

> "It's a story about a girl and her house fell... no wait a minute, her house went up. Well anyways, there was a witch, no um ... two witches and she wanted to go home and her dog ran out of the bicycle to a beautiful field with yellow flowers and little green munchkins. She had friends ... she had two friends; one had a heart, one was scared and one, hmm … I don't remember. She had beautiful red shoes. There was a yellow brick road but it wasn't really brick and they went to a wizard but he wasn't really a wizard."

What you will notice is that the child perpetually corrects him or herself. The child has great difficulty telling you what the main ideas of the story are. He or she also has trouble sequencing and telling you the order in which things happen. The child may get too immersed in the visual aspects of the story, for example the red shoes, the yellow brick road, that the story as a whole is not obvious or easily communicated. Please note that when these children are toddlers, they will routinely mispronounce and call things like spaghetti "pisghetti;" a dyslexic child often times does not grow out of this. You'll often hear words used like "whatchamacallit" or "thingamajig." There will be mispronunciations as well.

Following directions is another area of difficulty. Very often there is also left-right confusion. One of the main features of Dyslexia is that there is a broad span between low-functioning and high-functioning skills. For example, the dyscalculia person might have great difficulty with multiplication tables, but actually have a talent for doing high-level math such as calculus. The kids often hear, "How can someone as smart as you be so stupid?" They live in a world of contradictions. I have found that a good way of approaching the problem is to teach 'two steps backwards and one step ahead'. Let's say there is a first grade teacher who is introducing math to her class. The class has learned all of their addition AND subtraction facts. Once the addition and subtraction facts are memorized, she might think, "Wow, this is a really great class". She then proceeds to teach the class multiplication. With many dyslexics, the new information takes the place of or deletes the old information, thus the multiplication facts delete the addition facts. So when attempting to teach multiplication, it is best to use the Recursive Teaching Method, which is to review addition and subtraction facts once again, and then introduce the multiplication tables. More simply: review, review, and then move forward.

Dysnomia is another common form of Dyslexia. A person can study something for a test and know the material very well, but during the exam they cannot identify the correct words. What happened? It is as if they put the information into a filing cabinet in the brain, but they could not access that specific drawer they put it in. After the test, they can then access all the information. This form of Dyslexia is very uncomfortable. Dysnomia makes remembering certain things at the necessary time impossible. I will also know many songs and lyrics played on the radio, but if asked the name of the song or who's singing, I cannot tell you the answer.

I have noticed that there is another form of Dyslexia that has to do with people not being able to use technology such as computers, key components, Smartphones, and passwords. I would like to name this problem "Dystechnia." We did not need a name for this type of Dyslexia prior to the 1990s; it was a simpler time and technology didn't rule the world. People with this form of Dyslexia have a problem with computers, iPads and iPhones, which have become major aspects of modern society. Dystechnics have a general interference with technology overall. People reading this who have Dyslexia might be surprised or even delighted to find out that others have difficulty or much interference with technological gadgets.

On a positive note, dyslexics can often see things in an "out of the box" manner, using a different perspective. Many can take a three-dimensional object in their mind's eye and can rotate it, thereby seeing different angles. Often times inventors, designers, scientists, and architects have been able to create, not in spite of their Dyslexia but *because* of it. Famous dyslexics include Albert Einstein, Thomas Edison, Whoopie Goldberg, and Tom Cruise. These people went to high levels of their fields because of their abilities. When given the right support, Dyslexia is often a gift and a talent – a form of genius if you will. Leonardo Da Vinci, who lived from 1452 to 1519, and who was famous for painting the "Mona Lisa," "The Last Supper" and creating the Vitruvian Man, is believed by some to be dyslexic, because he would write right to left in mirror image in his notebooks. Most people do not know that drawings were discovered in his notebooks showing sketches of the helicopter engine and parts of a sewer system. It only took us five hundred years to create the helicopter and sewers that were sitting in his notebooks. It is because of Da Vinci's supposed Dyslexia and his ability to *visualize* that he was able to manipulate objects and create inventions so many years ahead of its time. Pablo Picasso had word blindness and is thought to have been possibly dyslexic as well.

Walt Disney is also considered to have had Dyslexia. It has been said that Walt Disney was fired from a job for being the most "untalented" and "uncreative" person a company ever had. He went on to create Mickey Mouse, Minnie Mouse, Disney World and changed the world through his creativity. Can you imagine for a moment a world without Disney? I certainly cannot.

Four presidents of the United States are believed to have had Dyslexia. These include George Washington, John F. Kennedy, Thomas Jefferson, and Woodrow Wilson. Other important dyslexics include Steve Jobs, Stephen Spielberg, Erin Brockovich, and Cher. Another notable fact is that Thomas Edison and Alexander Graham Bell, both dyslexics, made thousands of inventions, including both the telephone and the light bulb. Think about it for a moment; electricity is something that has always been around, but it took the brilliance of Edison to put it in the spotlight.

It is important for people who are dyslexic to find out what type of learner they are and have someone work with them to uncover their gifts. Many of the world's inventions have come from the mind, eye, and hand of a dyslexic.

Due to having undiagnosed Dyslexia as a child and only starting to read during my second year of college, I was compelled to keep this disability hidden. Having only learned to write during my Master's thesis, I eventually came to work with special needs kids because of my disability. Originally, I attempted to fulfill my Master's thesis with someone else writing while I spoke; my helper used the same words over and over again. Halfway through the assignment, I realized I could use the same words over and over again, too! I heard him use the words so many times, and it was such a profound moment for *me*. It is one of the major reasons why I have been able to create and provide recoveries within the pages of this book as well as in the lives of my clientele.

Chapter 5: Discovering Allergies and What to Do

As previously mentioned in an earlier chapter, food sensitivities and allergic reactions vary from the well-known common ways to very unusual ways. Lately many people have become sensitive or allergic to peanuts, wheat, gluten, food dyes, latex, milk and dairy, perfumes, cleaning products, silver fillings (amalgam), herbs, soaps, grass, trees, mold, and electronic devices. I will attempt to discuss sensitivities and allergies, starting with the more detrimental ones. The most noticeable symptoms are sometimes easy to ignore, which should obviously not be the case.

The Mayo Clinic states, "Food allergy is an immune system reaction that occurs soon after eating a certain food. Even a tiny amount of the allergy-causing food can trigger signs and symptoms such as digestive problems, hives, or swollen airways. In some people, a food allergy can cause severe symptoms or even a life-threatening reaction known as anaphylaxis" (2011). Anaphylaxis is defined as "a life-threatening emergency that requires an immediate epinephrine (adrenaline) shot and a trip to the emergency room." The Mayo Clinic says that "Anaphylaxis signs and symptoms include: constriction of airways, swollen throat, or a lump in your throat that makes it difficult to breathe, abdominal pain and cramping, rapid pulse, and shock (with a severe drop in blood pressure and felt as dizziness, lightheadedness, or loss of consciousness)."

Serum Sickness and Vaccines

In his article, *Vaccines and the Peanut Allergy Epidemic* (from *Spizz* magazine, July 2011), Dr. Tim O'Shea discusses the connection between allergies and vaccinations. Before 1900, anaphylactic shock was unknown in the medical field; sudden fainting, respiratory distress, convulsions, and death did not exist until the hypodermic needle replaced the lancet (a type of pricking device that does not penetrate deeply) during vaccinations. Right at that time, a variety of symptoms, including shock and death, suddenly resulted following an injection of a vaccine. This new condition was called Serum Sickness, claiming thousands of children. Serum Sickness was the first mass allergenic phenomenon in history. The connection between needles and serum sickness was well recognized and documented in the medical literature of the day.

When the needle replaced the lancet in the late 1800s, serum sickness soon became a known consequence of vaccinations. In fact, the early study of Serum Sickness coming from vaccines practically paved the way for the entire field of modern allergy medicine.

Early researchers like Claude Von Pirquet recognized that vaccines had two primary effects on the body: immunity and hypersensitivity; the latter came at the expense of the former. In fact, many doctors in the early 1900s were dead set against vaccines for this exact reason. Doctors like Walter Hadwen MD, and Alfred Russell Wallace kept meticulous records on how smallpox vaccines had actually increased the incidence of smallpox. After the inoculations, a good number of people died from the shots. "Within my long lifetime, its ruthless enforcement throughout Europe ended in two of the worst epidemics of smallpox in record, our former more dreaded typhus and cholera epidemics having meanwhile been ended by sanitation. After that failure, the credit of vaccination was saved for a while by the introduction of isolation, which at once produced improved figures. At present, intelligent people do not have their children vaccinated, nor does the law now compel them to. The result is not the extermination of the human race by smallpox; on the contrary more people are now killed by vaccination than by smallpox."-- George Bernard Shaw (August 9, 1944, the Irish Times).

Dr. Tim O'Shea's article states, "A researcher of the early 1900s, Dr Charles Richet (who coined the term *Anaphylaxis*) found that with food allergies the reaction came on as the result of intact proteins in the food having bypassed the digestive system and making their way intact into the blood, via leaky gut. The sudden violent reaction to food requires an initial sensitivity involving injection of some sort, followed by a later ingestion of the sensitized food. Get the shot, and then later eat the food. The initial exposure created the hypersensitivity. The second exposure would be the violent, perhaps fatal, physical event. Soon other doctors began to notice striking similarities between food reactions and the serum sickness that was associated with vaccines. Same exact clinical presentation."

The implications seem to have been forgotten today with the introduction of many allergens in children's vaccines.

Children before the age of two have still developing immune systems, which is thought to be affected by the presence of these allergens in vaccines.

Peanut Allergies

Peanut allergies have also risen dramatically in the past several decades. This condition brings the risk of asthmatic attack, shock, respiratory failure, and even death. Peanuts are a major cause of fatal and near fatal anaphylactic reaction to food. About 1% to 3% of the population has peanut and tree nut allergies.

Children from the fifties through the early eighties practically grew up on peanut butter and jelly sandwiches. Today many schools, camps, and cafeterias are roped off with signs saying "Peanut Free Zones." This situation causes many problems for our schools because it's incredibly difficult to monitor incoming peanut products. Even eating establishments have begun to stop leaving containers of peanuts out for the safety of allergic customers.

From the years of 1997 to 2008, families surveyed reported peanut allergies in children more than tripled nationally from 0.4% to 1.4% (according to a study published in the June 2010 issue of the *Journal of Allergy and Clinical Immunology*). It is important to note that the study also showed that there was "no significant increase" in adults. Other studies in Canada, Australia, and the UK show similar increases. According to a report from 2003, reported peanut allergies increased from 0.4% in 1997 to 0.8% in 2002 (Sicherer, Munoz-Furlong, and Sampson, 1206).

Many parents have been wondering where this great increase of peanut allergies came from, especially since no one in their family previously had peanut sensitivities before. What happened?

Over the past decade, people have been questioning a parallel increase in both the number of required immunization and the increase of food allergies. Some studies have shown that in communities where much less vaccinations were given to children under age two, the prevalence of peanut allergies was also low. Whereas in communities that had high vaccination rates the number of reported peanuts allergies were higher.

Heather Fraser researched allergic reactions to vaccines in her 2011 book *The Peanut Allergy Epidemic*. In her book, she discusses additives called Excipients, which were necessary to prolong the effect

of antibiotics when they are injected into the body, acting as carrier molecules. Without excipients, the benefits of penicillin would only last about two hours. It was found that refined oils worked best, acting as time-release capsules for the antibiotic. Peanut was chosen because it worked well and was inexpensive.

Soon enough, allergic reactions to penicillin became common, and it was recognized that this reaction was due to sensitivity to the excipient oils. That's what the allergy is – a sensitivity to the excipients. By 1950, antibiotics were given indiscriminately. Only then, in the 1950s, did peanut allergy begin to occur, even though Americans had been eating peanuts for well over a century. Then, peanut oils were introduced as vaccine excipients in the mid 1960s. Dr. O'Shea's article continues, "By 1980 they had become the preferred excipient. They were considered adjuvants – substances able to increase reactivity to the vaccine. This reinforced the Adjuvant Myth: the illusion that immune response is the same as immunity: the pretense being that the stronger the allergic response to the vaccine, the greater will be the immunity that is conferred. Historically, those researchers who challenged this Commandment of vaccine mythology did not advance their careers. The first study of peanut allergies was not undertaken until 1973. It was a study of peanut excipients in vaccines. Soon afterwards, and as a result of that study, manufacturers were no longer required to disclose all the ingredients in vaccines."

Dr. O'Shea further states, "The famous Maurice Hilleman found that even the most refined peanut oils still contained some traces of intact peanut proteins. This was the reason doctors were directed to inject vaccines intramuscular rather than intravenous – a greater chance of absorption of intact proteins, less chance of reaction. But that obviously wasn't enough to prevent sensitivity. The fundamental law of nature always applies: no intact proteins in the body."

In his article, Dr. O'Shea reviews Fraser's book, stating, "Although peanut allergies became fairly common during the 1980s, it wasn't until the early 1990s when there was a sudden surge of children reacting to peanuts – the true epidemic appeared. The Mandated Schedule of vaccines for children doubled from the 80s to the 90s:

1980 – 20 vaccines

1995 – 40 vaccines

2011 – 68 vaccines

It would be imprudent enough to feed peanuts to a newborn since their digestive system is largely unformed. But this is much worse – injecting intact proteins directly into the infant's blood. In 36 vaccines before the age of 18 months. As vaccines doubled between the 1980s and the 1990s, thousands of kids were now exhibiting peanut sensitivities, with many violent reactions that were sometimes fatal.

Following the next enormous increase in vaccines on the Mandated Schedule after 9/11 whereby the total shot up to 68 recommended vaccines, the peanut allergy soon reached epidemic proportions: a million children: 1.5% of them. These numbers fit the true definition of epidemic even though that word has never been used in mainstream literature with respect to peanut allergy, except in Fraser's book. Many researchers, not only Heather Fraser, could see very clearly that "The peanut allergy epidemic in children was precipitated by childhood injections."" (p106)

The reason peanuts are so allergenic is that peanuts are legumes, not really nuts, and contain Lectins, which are highly allergenic and harmful to the body. Furthermore, peanuts are susceptible to a mold that produces a Mycotoxin called Aflatoxin. Aflatoxin is a carcinogen that has been shown to cause liver cancer in rats (and, presumably, in humans). So it is not only the peanut's allergenic properties that are detrimental.

Peanut allergies are usually treated with an exclusion diet, in which the child is never exposed to peanuts. Parents must be vigilant about the avoidance of foods that may contain whole peanuts or peanut particles and/or oils. Peanut oils are found in some lotions as well, so parents have to be careful to also search the ingredients of these products.

Egg Allergies

Eggs are a complete protein and normally well digested by the body. Years ago people had eggs and other farm products delivered to the home. Back then, one barely ever heard of people having egg allergies. Somehow today eggs are one of the most common allergy-causing foods in children, affecting 1-2%. The allergy can be either to the egg yolk or to the white. Like all food allergies, symptoms range from mild reactions such as hives and nasal inflammation, to more severe ones such as vomiting and anaphylaxis. Cooking and heating the eggs seems to result in less of a reaction. This explains why some people react to lightly cooked or raw eggs and not to well cooked eggs. Some children are allergic to both.

The Mayo Clinic says, "Egg allergy reactions can vary from person to person and usually occur soon after exposure to egg. Egg allergy symptoms can include skin inflammation or hives (the most common egg allergy reaction), allergic nasal inflammation (allergic rhinitis), digestive (gastrointestinal) symptoms (such as cramps, nausea, and vomiting), and asthma signs and symptoms such as coughing, chest tightness, or shortness of breath." Eggs, like milk, are in a variety of foods, but can be tolerated by some if cooked properly. Parents must look carefully to investigate the ingredients of foods such as soups, pies, gravies, glazes on baked goods, Chinese fried rice, and other sources where it might not be obvious that eggs are an ingredient. Egg substitute products can be used.

The Mayo Clinic also states, "Egg allergy can occur as early as infancy." Once again, prior to the childhood bombardment of 70 or more different vaccines, there was a time when the average child suffered very few if any food allergies and had a limited occurrence of chronic illnesses. The author questions how so many of today's children became allergic to eggs in infancy. It is a fact that many vaccines are actually incubated in and with egg products. Is it any wonder why so many babies are affected? This situation is ironic because the pediatrician often tells the parents of an infant not to allow the baby to eat solid foods sometimes up to the age of 10-12 months and not to expose the baby to anything that might produce an allergen,

particularly not to eggs and peanuts; however, the vaccines recommended by the same doctors are conversely injecting the baby with eggs and peanuts. How contradictory is that? As a result, many more kids now have egg allergies. Being exposed to eggs at such a young age has created this problem. (Note: because of increasing complaints about the use of eggs in vaccine creation, some manufactures are instead using dog kidney cells. Perhaps we shall see a large increase in dog allergies in the near future?)

It is claimed that Measles vaccines are not grown in hen eggs, and therefore generally considered safe for egg allergic children. On the other hand, Influenza vaccines are often grown in egg cultures, so pro-vaccine people say that these vaccines should be given under the guidance of an allergist. Obviously, this idea is very impractical considering the authorization requirements of many medical health insurance plans and medical doctors.

Dairy Allergies

The skin is the largest organ in the human body. Observing the skin is one of the easiest ways to detect certain bodily issues. For example, a dairy sensitivity can be easily seen by way of the skin changing color and texture. A common symptom will be itchiness, as seen in eczema and psoriasis. These are often indications of undiagnosed milk allergies. Babies who have severe cradle cap, the raised peeling and pink blotches of skin, may be potentially experiencing a reaction from milk sensitivity or allergies. The simplest thing to do is to avoid feeding the child all dairy products for several weeks, to see if there is undiagnosed food sensitivity.

Similarly, if you are breastfeeding be careful to avoid eating milk and dairy products.

I cannot tell you how many times I have heard parents say that they have stopped exposing their child to dairy, but the skin did not get better. Frequently, this is because the parent switched the child from dairy to soy products without realizing that almost all milk-sensitive children (cheese is still a culprit, by the way) have soy sensitivity as well. If you are going to attempt to see if your child improves without dairy in their life, you must remove all soy products as well.

For older children, it is easier to determine whether or not they have food sensitivity. The easiest way to find out is to withhold the suspected item (all cheese, milk, butter, and soy products) for approximately four days.

On the fifth day, you want the child to have a lot of milk/dairy in his or her diet. An example would be having a breakfast of cereal with milk, lunch consisting of a grilled cheese sandwich oozing with cheese and ice cream for dessert. Top that off with a few slices of pizza for dinner, a glass of chocolate milk and more ice cream. Make an effort to do this when the children are off from school as you can monitor their responses better. What you will be looking for is to see any sudden reactions. If your child's skin suddenly gets bumpier, itchier and blotchier, you will know it was from a partial reaction to the milk. If your child also begins to experience intestinal issues such as diarrhea or constipation then you will know dairy was the culprit. If you find dairy to be problematic at times, but not overly serious, a small amount of milk without any kind of regularity, such as on a special event may be permissible. Milk on a regular basis at every meal is not.

Another thing that can be done in dealing with dairy allergies is to substitute Goat's milk instead of Cow or Soy milk. Goat's milk is believed to be more easily digestible and less allergenic than cow's milk. In the United States the most common food allergy for children under three is cow's milk. Mild side effects include vomiting, diarrhea, and skin rashes and severe effects can be as serious as anaphylactic shock! One fact is that goat's milk and human milk is only different by two proteins. Cow's milk is different by at least 12 proteins. Thus, goat's milk would be less allergenic. Unlike cow's milk, goat's milk does not contain agglutinin. As a result, the fat globules in goat's milk do not cluster together, making them easier to digest. Goat's milk does not need to be homogenized. The problem with homogenization is that once the cell wall of the fat globule has been broken, it releases a superoxide (free radical) known as Xanthine Oxidase. It is known that free radicals cause a host of problems in the body, the least of which is DNA mutations, which can lead to cancer.

Also, Goat's milk is low in essential fatty acids, like cow's milk, because goats also have Essential Fatty Acid destroying bacteria in their ruminant stomachs. Yet, goat milk is reported to contain more of the essential fatty acids Linoleic and Arachnodonic Acids, in addition to a higher proportion of short-chain and medium-chain fatty acids. These are easier for intestinal enzymes to digest. Goat's milk has greater amounts of vitamin B-6, vitamin A, and niacin and is

a far superior source of the vitally important nutrient potassium. Goat's milk protein also makes softer curds (the term given to the protein clumps that are formed by the action of your stomach acid on the protein), which again makes them easier to digest rapidly. This would greatly help infants and children who regurgitate cow's milk easily. Goat's milk contains slightly lower levels of lactose (4.1 percent versus 4.7 percent in cow's milk), and therefore is easier to digest for those suffering from lactose intolerance.

When it comes to allergies, goat's milk may also have other advantages. Goat's milk contains only trace amounts (89% less) of an allergenic casein protein, alpha-S1, found in cow's milk. Goat's milk casein is more similar to human milk. In fact a recent study of infants allergic to cow's milk found that nearly 93% could drink goat's milk with virtually no side effects. Many mothers report no ear aches in their children as well, unlike when their children drank cow's milk. Finally, goat's milk is better for human consumption. A baby usually starts life at around 7-9 pounds, a baby goat (kid) usually starts life at around 7-9 pounds, and a baby cow (calf) usually starts life at around 100 pounds. Now speaking from a purely thermodynamic position, these two animals have very significant and different nutritional needs for both maintenance and growth requirements. Cow's milk is designed to take a 100 pound calf and transform it into a 1200 pound cow. Goat's milk and human milk were both designed and created for transforming a 7-9 pound baby/kid into an average adult/goat of anywhere between 100-200 pounds. Thus, goat's milk is less

allergenic, naturally homogenized, easier to digest, lactose intolerant friendly, and biochemically/thermodynamically superior to cow's milk. For more information see: www.mtcapra.com/benefits-of-goat-milk-vs-cow-milk

Gluten Allergies

Gluten allergies are the "new kids on the block." Gluten is found in wheat, barley, rye, and in some oats. Researchers point out that gluten disorders are most common in Caucasian people and those with a European ancestry; women are affected more than men. In some, the inability to digest gluten is identified as life threatening and is related to Celiac disease and in others the inability to digest gluten is showing up in large numbers amongst people who have different types of inflammation, such as arthritis. People with Celiac and/or gluten sensitivity are more likely to have autoimmune disorders such as Rheumatoid Arthritis, Systemic Lupus, and Sjogren's Syndrome (another form of Arthritis).

According to the *A.D.A.M. Medical Encyclopedia*, Celiac is "a condition that damages the lining of the small intestine and prevents it from absorbing parts of food that are important for staying healthy. The damage is due to a reaction to eating gluten, which is found in wheat, barley, rye, and possibly oats" (Dugdale, Longstreth, & Zieve, 2010).

The website continues with, "The exact cause of celiac disease is unknown. The lining of the intestines contains areas called Villi, which help absorb nutrients. When people with celiac disease eat foods or use products that contain gluten, their immune system react by damaging these Villi. This damage affects the ability to absorb nutrients properly. A person becomes malnourished, no matter how much food he or she eats. The disease can develop at any point in life, from infancy to late adulthood."

In fact, many health practitioners believe that nearly all inflammation is connected to gluten intolerance. Perhaps the reader has noticed by now how many times we are told that a certain illness or disease is a mystery or a puzzle; in fact, the logo for many Autism sites is a missing puzzle piece. Here, we are told that the cause of Celiac is unknown, yet there was almost no Celiac before the escalation of vaccines. This pattern is troubling.

Growing up, I had never heard of anyone with gluten intolerance. By the 1990s it became common. Adults who could previously digest gluten and do not have Celiac are suddenly becoming ill from the gluten. Just a few years ago, few had heard of Celiac or gluten intolerance, but now gluten- free foods are becoming more common in grocery stores. Gluten-free foods are typically more expensive than regular food, but when your child has a gluten allergy, you can hardly take them out to eat. It is like being trapped in your own home. Trying to take them to a Chinese restaurant is a risk. Not just for the peanuts and peanut oil, but the flours and other additives used to thicken the sauces which usually contain gluten. There are many hidden sources of gluten. Even some vitamin and mineral supplements will have gluten as a filler in them. It is essential to their very survival that children with celiac are not exposed to wheat or gluten of any kind.

Celiac, at this point in time, is not supposedly curable. Some doctors will treat Celiac with Corticosteroids (i.e., Prednisone), but in some cases Celiac Sprue does not respond well to treatment. Prednisone has a host of bad side effects. Again, a proper diet or even a fast should be able to jump-start the gluten-free diet and put a hold to the symptoms. However, your symptoms may go away and the Villi in the lining of the intestines can be healed if you follow a lifelong gluten-free diet which includes not ingesting foods, drinks, and medications that contain wheat, barley, rye, and possibly oats.

More and more people are also becoming intolerant of wheat and wheat products partly because of the rise of foods being genetically modified and altered. Celiac Disease is a case where seeing a naturopath or homeopath could be of the utmost importance, especially since traditional medicine offers few alternatives or choices.

One of the biggest things that have come along for autistic children is the GFCF diet, which stands for Gluten-Free Casein-Free diet; this has become a very popular first line of defense for autistic families. According to the website GFCFDiet.com, "the GFCF Diet is one of the very first recommendations made by the Autism Research Institute. It is considered to be a cornerstone of the DAN Approach"[vii]. Many parents report improvements in symptoms of Autism with this diet, but once again little research has been done by the scientific community because the majority of all the research has come from the pharmaceutical enterprises. Sorry to say this, but the impetus to study the benefits of children who are placed on

a GFCF diet is not there because they can simply choose to stop ingesting gluten rather than take another vaccine or a pill. By changing the diet, many problems are averted so there would be little reason for the pharmaceuticals to make money.

Seafood and Shellfish Allergies

Seafood and shellfish allergies are on the rise too. Seafood allergy means it is an allergy towards the proteins found in types of seafood, such as fish and shellfish. The Mayo Clinic says, "Shellfish include marine animals with shells, such as shrimp, crab, and lobster". You might be surprised to find that they include octopus and squid with shellfish allergies. The Mayo Clinic concludes that a "Shellfish allergy can cause mild symptoms, such as hives or nasal congestion, or more-severe and even life-threatening symptoms. For some people, even a tiny amount of shellfish can cause a serious reaction" (Mayo Clinic staff, 2011). According to the website featuring the Kid's Health fact sheets: http://kidshealth.schn.health.nsw.gov.au/

"Many allergic reactions to seafood are mild and consist of hives around the mouth where seafood has touched the skin, or more generalized hives on other parts of the body. Abdominal pain and vomiting after eating seafood may also occur as part of an allergic reaction. More sensitive children can develop coughing, wheeze, difficulty breathing or hoarseness of the voice due to an allergic reaction occurring in the throat and breathing tubes. This reaction is known as anaphylaxis. In the most severe cases collapse and loss of consciousness can occur.

Steam and vapors from seafood may cause wheezing or hay fever-like symptoms (runny nose, sneezing, itchy eyes) in some children. These children do not appear to be more at risk of anaphylaxis.

Not every adverse reaction to seafood is caused by an allergic reaction. Some reactions can resemble allergic reactions but are actually caused by contaminants present in the seafood."

Parents need to be careful about cross contamination from items that were previously touching a dish or pan that held seafood as this situation will cause a reaction as well. Also, it can be found in some medicines, so vigilance is highly necessary. Shellfish can be mixed in with fish by-products, which are used to make fish oil.

Squalene, which is made from Sharks, has been found in Flu, Tetanus, Pertussis, and other vaccines (see chart in Chapter 1). People having severe reactions to Tetanus shots as adults seem to have had such reactions to their DPT shots during infancy. Numbers of these people also have seafood allergies as well.

Food Dye Sensitivities

Food dyes were originally intended for use in the making of asphalt streets, they are tar and petroleum based products.

There has been an explosive amount of artificial food dyes such as red dye #40, blue dye #1, and yellow #5 that have caused sensitivities. Yellow #5 is also known as Tartrazine and may be found in some cosmetics, vitamins, and prescription medications. These dyes are added to cereals, ice cream, candies, juices, sodas, toothpaste, and many other products. In fact, I would venture to say that the majority of all commercially processed food has these fake colors added. In fact, the Blue #2 that dyes jeans is also used for foods. Food dyes made from petroleum are often hidden and not labeled, oranges are sprayed with citrus red dye to appear more nutritious, supermarket beef is injected with red dye to hide its grey appearance, and salmon is fed red dyed feed to alter its flesh color.

There are children who have one bite of a food with dye and react within a few minutes to 24 hours later. They may have eczema, bedwetting, tantrums, fits, mood swings, or become aggressive. At first it might appear that they have become upset for a certain reason such as not being able to find a toy, but instead, they are actually having a full blown chemical reaction. Sometimes there are hidden food dye reactions, for example Tartrazine can cause migraines, depression, hives, blurred vision, heatwaves, purple skin patches, and sleep disruptions. Dyes also have been linked to asthma attacks, hyperactivity, and thyroid tumors.

As a parent, it is best that every ingredient is read. Even when you take the time to read the labels, you still cannot be sure that food dyes have not been added. This confusion is because there are loopholes in the food labeling laws that allow companies to omit food coloring ingredients from the labels. For example, a soy sauce packet does not need to list the dye. Other products may have as many as five different dyes to make the food appear as if it has natural coloring. Another example would be when purchasing two different brands of marshmallows; one may list blue dye #1 while the other may not. Usually, one cannot tell the difference, both are white in appearance.

The only pickles I have found in a regular food store not to contain dye is a brand called Claussons. Even most children's juice boxes contain dye. The purpose is obscure because the children can't see the color of the juice in the box. There are many artificial dyes in medicines such as children's Tylenol and Motrin that are bright pink and orange.

There are products on the market such as Motrin Dye Free, Tylenol Dye Free, if you choose to eliminate intake of dyes. Even common items such as toothpaste and mouthwash contain dyes.

There was a study done in England in 2004 on the effects of food dyes on children. During the study, so many children reacted negatively to the dyes that the study had to be discontinued. Over the next few years it was decided that no food dyes would be permitted whatsoever in the UK because of such clear findings. In the UK it was decided that warning labels would be placed on all items containing dyes, instead. The warnings say that the dyes may cause hyperactivity in some children, "consumption may have an adverse effect on activity and attention in children". It is similar to the surgeon general's warning on a box of cigarettes. A

2007 study by the British Food Standards Agency linked food dyes with increased levels of hyperactivity, ADHD, and also lower IQs in typical/ordinary children. By 2009, all dyes were removed from British food products.

In the USA, similar studies somehow came to a different conclusion. A claim was made that the dyes only affect a portion of the population and thus it is not necessary to publish this warning. It is the pharmaceutical industry and food dye industry that conducted these studies. How strange that children can get sick overseas over food dyes, but not here. We are actually 10 to 20 years behind the UK.

It seems as if food dye use has become an insurmountable problem. The original intent of dying the foods was to have people be more attracted to it. Instead, people are getting sick over it.

Hospitals use it too, and it becomes down right dangerous. Food tubes used in hospitals are often differentiated from medicine tubes with blue dye so that hospital staff can tell them apart. Sometimes this can accelerate the death of an ill patient. These additives are indeed dangerous.

So much complicated work is done in the US to raise test scores and IQs for school children, but perhaps we should go back to basics such as making sure food is healthy by removing food dyes, especially in school lunches.

Seasonal Allergies

People often assume that seasonal allergies run in families. They believe that seasonal allergies are inherited. While it may be true for some, it is not true for all. There exists an underlying condition that affects seasonal allergies, food allergies, and pet allergies. That common thread is Candida or a yeast infection as mentioned in previous chapters. The human body has the capacity to handle some allergens but when there are too many, the body breaks down. Thus, having yeast plus allergies is equivalent to pouring water into a glass to the point where it overflows.

During the rainy season, the child might sniffle, wheeze, and get worse every fall season. Damp falling leaves from a tree will start to produce mold and fungus and exacerbate allergy reactions. Damp musty basements, mold around the shower, all can contribute to the illness and overall malaise of the child.

Forced air from a damp basement can make the situation intolerable. The child becomes over sensitive to dust mites, mold, condensation in the air, and musty smells. Also affecting the child are perfumes and the scent to cleaning products. Laundry detergents, soaps, and fabric softeners can make the child feel worse. It is not that the child can't handle a little laundry detergent by itself; it is the cumulative effect of these chemicals and irritants that causes the 'water to overflow from the glass'.

Latex Allergies

There is one type of allergy that took me almost three decades to realize it. Working with children one-on-one, I have often come across kids who erase more on their paper than write. I have seen children spend an hour on their homework with close to nothing done. At times, they erase so feverishly that they put holes in the paper. As the result of some children having intense allergy testing, I have now come to understand that this behavior and problem is often a result of a chemical allergy. That allergy is to latex, which is found in pencil erasers. I am not sure if they're erasing like that to release the smell or if the smell makes them agitated, but whatever it is, the behaviors are crystal clear. I can just hear some of the parents of these children, sitting at the table with their child, begging, "just finish the sentence, please."

Latex can be found in balloons as well. I do not remember if it was I who coined the phrase or if I heard it somewhere else, but for many years I have been using the term "erase-itis." You may be surprised to learn that you can purchase "latex-free" pencils in places such as Staples and Wal-Mart, as well as stationary stores. You may also be surprised to learn that the workers in the local stores have absolutely no idea what a latex-free pencil is or that their store is

even selling it. A couple of times I have spoken with store managers or have had telephone conversations with a superior and they too are unaware that they carried a "latex-free" supply.

I once came across a young lady suffering from stomach aches and unusual rashes; it appeared to be a horizontal bull's-eye rash similar to the kind you would find from a tick bite with Lyme disease. It turned out that she was having a reaction to the latex at the top of her waistband of her outfit.

Other Types of Allergies

It is my experience that a number of these various allergies left unattended, coupled with perfumes and chemical scents, can lead to asthma. There are some that say that asthma is the first step of anaphylactic shock. With asthma, the child can barely breathe. It is as if air will not get into the lungs. Serious asthma can land the child in an emergency room. Strong prescription medications such as inhalers with Albuteral Sulfate are often given. I cannot tell how many times I have heard on the news, "the U.S. Government is looking into why there is so much asthma in inner city youth" or "scientists are researching why so many children are afflicted with asthma". It always surprises me that they pretend not to know. It is this soup of vaccines, antibiotics, food allergies, chemicals, creating an allergy vortex that leads to large numbers of asthmatic children and adults.

A study in *Epidemiology* (1997 Nov;8(6):678-80) cites "Is infant immunization a risk factor for childhood asthma or allergy? This study followed 1,265 children born in 1977. The 23 children who received no DPT and polio immunizations had no recorded asthma episodes or consultations for asthma or other allergic illness before age 10 years; in the immunized children, 23.1% had asthma episodes, 22.5% asthma consultations, and 30% consultations for other allergic illness. Similar differences were observed at ages 5 and 16 years." PMID 9345669

When it comes to a chronically ill child with a plethora of food and chemical sensitivities, nothing should be taken for granted. I once knew a child who sucked on Hall's Breezes lozenges and did fine when having a sore throat. One day, they switched to the Natural Hall's Breezes and within a few hours, the child developed hives all over his body and started to swell up. Despite a couple of Benadryl, the swelling continued to take over. The boy was rushed to the hospital, looking like he had a bad case of the measles. It turned out that he was allergic to one of the herbal ingredients in the "natural" Hall's Breeze's product. The ER staff proceeded to inject him several times with epinephrine before the swelling and hives subsided, and he was sent home.

Another instance occurred some thirty years ago when I was in the Florida Keys. In order to not get sun poisoning, I used a product called PreSun. I ended-up looking like a zebra; it appeared as if I applied it with spread fingers. The next day, I re-applied the product and in a short time, I looked lobster-red. At the local medical clinic, the doctor took one look at me and announced he knew exactly what the problem was. It was poisoning from the sun block. It may have been "manmade" Pabas, but whatever it was a

series of epinephrine injections sufficed and I was good to go.

We have come to the point as a society where almost nothing can be taken for granted when it comes to our children's health. It is a strange group of chemical sensitivities that have emerged as a result of decades of plastics, vaccines, dangerous fluorides, air chemicals, pesticides, emissions, GMO, and nano-particles that most don't know even exist, they all seem to have sped-up the process of deterioration. The ultimate purpose of this chapter is to make a positive shift away from this 'chemicalized' world to go the long way around to get to the shortcut; in this case, it means getting back to pure food, pure water, and other basics.

Chapter 6: Detoxifying

When trying to recover your child, detoxification is among one of the most important steps to take. There are many methods and it is truly complex, but once we identify the different aspects of the problem, it can become simpler.

Chelation Therapy

Chelation is one method for detoxification. Chelation comes from the Greek word "Chele," which means a claw, giving the idea of grabbing. Chelation therapy has a long history of use in clinical toxicology. Chelation involves using intravenous, oral, or rectal chelating agents for removing lead, arsenic, aluminum, mercury, cadmium, nickel, and other metals from the blood vessels and other parts of the body. Chelation agents bind to heavy metals so that they can be removed from the body. This would reduce the toxic reactions. The claim is that Chelation also improves circulation while reducing the symptoms of arthritis, diabetes, high blood pressure, and eye diseases such as macular degeneration. Chelation is done under the supervision of a doctor.

The human body is not designed to digest and decompose metals; some metals need massive amounts of fire and heat before they melt. The body doesn't have the amount of energy that a roaring fire would have without depleting its basic energy.

Chelating agents bind to and remove heavy metals from the body, which has been having outstanding benefits in a large number of children with Autism and some with ADHD as well. Remember that these heavy metal toxins are being injected into your newborn baby.

For example, many autistic children seem to have higher levels than normal of mercury retained in the body. Both Autism and mercury exposure are characterized by functional impairment to speech, language, and behavior (Bernard 2001, Blaxill 2004b). Recent studies also suggest that the same key regions of the brain are affected in both cases (Limke 2004, Kates 2004).

Mercury is a known neurotoxin and was regularly found in vaccines prior to 2002. It was claimed by the manufacturers that mercury was replaced by low-mercury or "thimerosal-free" vaccines. Instead, aluminum was added as the mercury content was reduced.

Aluminum is one of the metals that are removed via Chelation. It has been implicated for many years as a factor in the causation of Alzheimer's disease.

Aluminum salt is a very powerful adjuvant found in some vaccines with little study done about its safety. This poisonous metal can disrupt normal biochemical processes.

Giving babies multiple rounds of vaccines containing Aluminum gives them exposure that is many times more than is safe. The website thinktwice.com shows the following information that was taken directly from the manufacturers product inserts:" . . . for a 6 pound baby, 11-14mcg would be toxic. The Hepatitis B vaccine given at birth contains 250mcg of aluminum – 20 times higher that safety levels. Babies weigh about 12 pounds (5.5kg) at two months of age when they receive 1,225mcg of aluminum from their vaccines – 50 times higher than safety levels."

According to a study accessed through the website PubMed.gov, an open-label observational study was done. They state, "This study examined 10 children aged 4-10 years old who had been diagnosed with both Autistic Spectrum Disorder and ADHD by outside physicians or psychologists. These 10 children presented consecutively in an environmental medicine clinic in Buffalo, New York. The children were given comprehensive nutritional/ environmental/ Chelation treatment for 3 to 6 months in addition to their usual behavioral, educational, speech, and physical therapies" (Patel & Curtis, 2007). The study concludes "All 10 children showed significant improvement in many areas of social interaction, concentration, writing, language, and behavior. Urinary lead burden dropped significantly in all 10 children."

According to John Green, M.D. on the Autism Research Institute website, who was also a Defeat Autism Now (DAN) doctor, "There is strong evidence that autistic children have impairments in their body detoxification systems, causing increased vulnerability to toxic injury. In addition to heavy metals (particularly mercury, lead, arsenic, antimony, and aluminum), we have found elevated blood levels of PCBs and volatile organic solvents in every autistic child tested in our office. These toxins further weaken their detoxification systems, by causing oxidative injury, immune dysfunction, the impairment of enzyme and energy functions, disruption of cellular communications, and initiation and aggravation of chronic inflammation. The result of these disturbances is a complex set of self-perpetuating cycles of tissue injury. Detoxification by Chelation and attendant supportive treatments helps break these cycles and restore healthy physiology" (Green, 2006).

According to the paper "*Mercury Detoxification*" written in February 2005, "During the past year, a number of physicians from throughout the United States who have been working with autistic children have reported extremely good results in improving the health and behavior of autistic children when the mercury in the children's bodies were removed by a systematic process of detoxification. Some of these physicians, who have specialized in the treatment of autistic children for a number of years, and who have treated many hundreds of autistic children, report that no other treatment has brought about the remarkable improvement that they have

seen in many cases of mercury detoxification. Detoxification is not simple, and there are many competing detoxification protocols," (Autism Research Institute, 2005)[viii].

To this day, medical professionals are running conferences throughout the U.S. that seek to arrange for the best, safest Chelation methods available.[ix] While there are medical experts who perform what is known as "Chelation Therapy," as in anything, there are some concerns regarding this. The author would like parents to know that there have been some reports of children dying from IV Chelation therapy – a rigorous procedure – but that it was found that incorrect medications and methods were accidently used.

Natural Methods used for Detoxifying

While there are stories where dangerous pills or injections were used to detox an autistic child from mercury, we've also heard of other miraculous detoxifications that have contributed to recovery from illness. There are other ways to start the safe detoxification of your child.

Mercury is also found in dental fillings, which leaches into the body. Dentists can remove the amalgam fillings that contain mercury and replace them with mercury free fillings. There are dentists who specialize in removing them safely. They use oxygen masks, gloves, and other measures so that you do not ingest the mercury.

There are other safe and gentle ways of doing something like Chelation from the comfort of your own home. Some detoxification methods you can do include the use of clay baths, Epsom salts, baking soda, as well as using natural unbleached sea salt added to the bath water. All these products aid in detoxifying the body when used in baths. They pull out foreign substances from the pores, the soles of the feet, and so on. It is said that most poisons are positively charged, thus the use of clay and other baths - whose particles are negatively charged - may draw out these poisons to leave the body.

Epsom salt baths have long been used to draw out toxins from the body. This occurs during the first 15 minutes of the bath, after which time this water needs to be discarded or it can be reabsorbed into the body. According to Epsom Salt Council, "Epson salt is made up of magnesium and sulfate, which can improve health in numerous ways. A lack of magnesium – which helps regulate the activity of more than 300 enzymes in the body – can contribute to high blood pressure, hyperactivity, heart problems, and other health issues, doctors warn. Sulfate is essential for many biological processes. It helps to flush toxins and form proteins in joints, brain tissue, and Mucin proteins" (Epsom Salt Council, 2012). The mineral Magnesium is a potent detoxifier because it is used in many detox pathways and is contained naturally in kelp and sea salt. Minerals such as magnesium are also essential to help rebuild the digestive and immune systems in a child with Autism reacting from environmental causes.

Detoxification via Vitamins and Minerals

It is important to consider organic foods and adding trace minerals to the diet
126
that have been depleted from our agricultural and food industry. Many people believe that they don't need vitamins and minerals because they already eat a balanced diet. The problem is that commercial farms have been using the same fields for their vegetable crops over and over, thereby depleting precious trace minerals from the soil that the body needs for optimal health; they have been farmed in the same fields for nearly a century. Also, the water that has been transported to the farms contains poisonous fluoride, pesticides, antibiotics, drugs, etc.

In 2004, according to the website cncahealth.com, University of Texas biochemist Donald Davis, PhD analyzed a US Department of Agriculture report on 43 common garden fruits and vegetables and found that almost half of the substances containing minerals important

Recovering Autism, ADHD, & Special Needs

to proper health had lost nutritional value. They study shows that six out of 13 nutrients showed reliable declines between 1950 and 1999. Declines ranged from 6% to 38%.

To have a well enhanced diet, eating garlic, onions, cilantro, and curcumin is recommended. These foods play a big part in removing toxins from the body. Onion is said to clean the blood. Garlic protects blood immune-stimulant, supplies sulfur, is anti-parasitic, and anti-microbial. Garlic activates phagocytes that destroy invading microbes as well as B-cells and T-cells. Curcumin is purported to have a variety of things to fight cancers. Also, Chlorella and Spirulina, freshwater 'seaweeds', are also useful in removing heavy metals.

There is some exciting research done with things such as Glutathione.

Glutathione is an antioxidant that is reported to detox mercury, lead, and arsenic; as we age we lose some of our Glutathione. By replacing the lost Glutathione, we improve our liver, and mental and immune functions, as well as increase our energy. New reports also suggest that it is helpful against cancer. Children on the autistic spectrum have lower levels of Glutathione. Dr. Gustavo Baughman, a retired professor at McGill University in Montreal, Canada says it is the body's most important antioxidant because it is found within the cell.

The skin is our largest organ and sweating helps to secrete toxins. Raising body temperature with things like infrared light saunas can help kill parasites, viruses, and fungus, which some people have trouble eliminating due to hypothyroid conditions. The skin also helps make important nutrients through the absorption of sunlight.

Vitamins also do wonders for the body. According to Dr. Mercola, "the farther you live from the equator, the higher the risk of developing high blood pressure." He also says, "blood pressure is higher during the winter months than it is during the [summer.] Sunlight actually affects blood pressure in several ways. Sun exposure causes your body to produce Vitamin D. Lack of sunlight reduces your Vitamin D stores, and increases parathyroid hormone production, which increases blood pressure" (Mercola, How You Can Normalize Your Blood Pressure Without Drugs, 2009).

Dr. Mercola also states, "Vitamin D deficiency has been linked to insulin resistance, syndrome-X (also known as metabolic syndrome) … and other health problems including elevated cholesterol, triglyceride levels, obesity, and high blood pressure. Additionally, exposure to UV rays is thought to cause the release of endorphins, chemicals in your brain that produce feelings of euphoria and relief from pain and naturally relieve stress." Dr. Mercola cautions people to be careful about getting a prescription for Vitamin D from your doctor because generally it is for Vitamin D2, which is synthetic and our bodies really need D3.

According to the Office of Dietary Supplements (2011), "Vitamin D promotes calcium absorption in the gut and maintains adequate serum calcium and phosphate concentrations to enable normal mineralization of bone and to prevent hypocalcemic tetany (decreased blood calcium level with continuous tonic spasm of a muscle). It is also needed for bone growth and bone remodeling by Osteoblasts and Osteoclasts. Without sufficient vitamin D, bones can become thin, brittle, or misshapen. Vitamin D sufficiency prevents rickets in children and Osteomalacia in adults. Together with calcium, vitamin D also helps protect older adults from Osteoporosis". They also state that, "Vitamin D has other roles in the body, including modulation of cell growth, neuromuscular and immune function, and reduction of inflammation."

After reviewing the chart on the Office of Dietary Supplements website that stated everyone – both male and female – from the ages of one through 70 requires 600 IUs. For pregnant females who are lactating, the chart claims it is also 600 IUs. Upon further inspection, they have a table of selected food sources of Vitamin D and the very first food that is

listed is one tablespoon of cod liver oil having 1,360 IUs. Another example is sword fish (3 oz., cooked), which has 566 IUs. Notice the contradiction between the 600 IUs and 1,360 IUs. I am asking you, the consumer, to think!

One of the simplest and most important things is to keep your vitamin D3 level high. It is not to be confused with synthetic vitamins D1 or D2. D3 is more of a hormone than a vitamin. It is sold in the vitamin section of your health food store. It is the natural component that we get when we are out in sunshine. In the past 20 years or so, we have been told to stay out of the sun and slather ourselves with sun blocking lotions to prevent skin cancer. Consequently, most Americans are lacking this essential component. When tested as a group, children on the autistic spectrum have tremendously low amounts of D3, even when exposed to sunshine.

Some believe that glutathione is an important component of the body's ability to use D3. My belief is that children with Autism and ADHD have difficulty processing the amount of D3 that is needed for optimal health. Many have noticed how the rate of cancer alone in the United States has shot up in the last 20 years. I suspect that the lack of vitamin D3 one of the reasons. Doctors and scientists such as Dr. Mercola and Dr. Eisenstein speak of it regularly! All systems of the body require D3. Many believe that it is particularly effective in preventing cancers. It is time for us to go back into the sunshine. Countries where people are out in the sun all day have relatively little cancer, an example of this would be Jamaica. We have this backwards. Colds and flues occur more often because of this.

They occur less during the warm months. Further anecdotal evidence can be thought of that people get sick more often during the cold and winter months due to a lack of sun exposure and consequently D3.

It is interesting to note that while D3 is a very inexpensive hormone/ vitamin, some doctors have taken to writing prescriptions for up to 50,000 IUs for their patients, which is a confusing contradiction. On the one hand, doctors and pharmaceutical companies are uninspired about the benefits of vitamins but then go to the extreme of writing *prescriptions* for 50,000 IUs of D3. The message here is that it is NOT OK for you to freely go to a store and purchase an inexpensive vitamin for your health being told it may not be safe, but it is OK for you to get a prescription to get a large dose at one time, and get told it IS good for your health. And this is at the very core of this book; this is the very predicament that we have been put in.

D3 is the master of all vitamins. It seems to accelerate and/or make other vitamins work efficiently. It is not surprising to me that this generation of autistic, ADHD, and learning-disabled children is sicklier as they have been taught to stay out of the sun. Either by accident or on purpose, they have been placed in many supervised class programs and kept primarily indoors. It is equally not surprising to look at how our cancer epidemic has escalated. We are the most sun-deprived and sun-blocked consumers on earth and it is time to turn it around.

BPA Contamination

Today, people are finally learning about the poison that is leaking from plastic products and the lining of cans under the name Bisphenol A (BPA). This chemical was reported in 2008 by several governments questioning its safety. In 2010 a report from the FDA raised concerns regarding the exposure of fetuses, infants, and young children to BPA[x]. BPA can cross the placenta from mother to fetus, which leaves the fetus unprotected (as noted in Environmental Health News, June 7, 2010). The EU and Canada have declared BPA a toxic substance and have banned it from baby bottles.

The truth is that this chemical has been around since the fifties[xi]. It is during this time our exposure to Phalates and BPA increased. The "Tupperware generation" took hold after World War II and convenience items were advertised boldly in television and in magazines. The body cannot digest these plastics and it is increasing our toxic overload. The use of these plastics is now as American as apple pie, but it comes at a heavy price.

Even aluminum cans are lined with BPA and Poly-Bromenated Diphenyl Ethers (PBDEs). The chemicals leak endocrine disrupting compounds that have been linked to significant hormonal changes. These hormone disrupters have lead to the feminizing of males. This first came to my attention some 30 years ago when I read reports showing that there were fish in the UK downstream from major plastics factories that were dumping waste into the river. Suddenly all the fish turned female and were able to lay eggs without the presence of males. An entire section of a species' population turning female led the author to realize that there would be many side effects in the future..

Attempting to detox from the plastics and cans would be a benefit. BPA is used in polycarbonate plastics, thermal receipts, and food can linings; Phthalates are found in cosmetics, personal care products, and vinyl plastics. Both are instrumental in making plastic flexible. A Mount Sinai Children's environmental health study showed that pregnant women exposed to endocrine disrupting chemicals experience interference with hormone regulation (Braun, 2011). When you stop and think about it, even the vaccine syringes are made of plastic and may contain Phthalates and BPA.

It is not that I am suggesting that you refrain from using plastic products all the time, which is near impossible today. Instead, I suggest that you *reduce* the use of plastics whenever possible. The easiest way to do this is to save food in glass jars.

Pickle jars work especially well as they have a wide mouth, are easy to wash, and are useful for storage. If you insist on reheating something in the microwave, it is best to use a glass or Corningware container. Another easy step to take is to stop purchasing drinking water in plastic bottles. They leech BPA and fill up our landfills. While there are new forms of plastic being created that claim to be "BPA-free", we still don't know the long term safety of the chemicals in the newer plastics. For now, it is best to move toward glass and stainless steel containers.

The fertility of our population is also adversely affected; 35 years ago, it would have been rare to see a fertility clinic. Today, there is one in every major city and in most suburbs. Why? The answer is because we need them. We have turned the corner for all mankind. This is the first time since the dawn of humanity that men and women needed help getting pregnant or keeping the baby in the womb until the proper time. Male sperm, from the 1960s to today, has only approximately 25% of it still alive, swimming and well. If this is all due to breakthroughs in modern technology and science, *who needs it?* There is a turning point where technology / science has become destructive, rather than constructive. This correlates with a general system-wide failure in many of our structures from finance, politics, and education, to resolve this climate of co-inability. Corporate profits are placed above the average person's wellbeing, and all are now suffering. We all need to simply go back to the very basics. We need to work from our hearts and from love, not from our heads.

Detoxifying from environmental toxins can be as simple as eating garlic, cilantro, and increasing vitamin therapy and are extraordinary steps that you can take for family's safety. Detoxifying from mercury and other heavy metals can also be done, but require the support of knowledgeable health professionals.

Chapter 7: Remedies and Treatments

There are a myriad of simple natural remedies and treatments for various ailments that may affect special needs children, some of which have been around for hundreds of years but did not make it into mainstream allopathic medicine of today. In this chapter, the more accessible the remedy and the simpler it is to use, the better.

Bowel Issues

Many children on the Autism spectrum have intermittent bouts of diarrhea and constipation. As soon as the constipation is gone, the diarrhea shows up. What seems to be happening is that due to the high levels of stress set off by the slightest changes and transitions, these children tend to clamp up and squeeze their abdominal area / guts. Such children overreact to their environment and their nervous systems are in a "fight or flight" response most of the time for the smallest little things. Just asking them to brush their teeth will cause such reactions. As a result, these children tend to hold their breath, squeeze all their muscles and organs, tighten their fists, grimace their face and grunt a lot. The act of repeatedly contracting seems to affect their stomach, colon, and intestines. It is well known that children on the spectrum have more gut and bowel disorders than other children.

In these situations, the food traveling through the small intestine does not get fully digested and causes irritation of the lining. Then the large particles of undigested food enter into the colon. The colon clamps down when stressing and contracting and pieces of undigested food and fecal matter seem to get stuck, forming a clump. While the pieces are stuck, the only substance that can pass around it is liquid matter; so, typically a child can have blistering diarrhea for several days. Eventually, the hard matter shrinks and then slowly makes its way out. Therefore, the child suddenly goes from blistering diarrhea to hard and compacted constipation. It goes from one extreme to the other and can be extremely detrimental to the child's health. These kids tend not to have regular and normal bowel movements. After days of uncomfortable diarrhea, a parent will often take their child to a pediatrician to explain the symptoms only to find out that in the past few hours, it has turned into a problem of severe constipation or likewise, the other way around. This condition is very similar to Colitis or Irritable Bowel Syndrome.

Within the Autism community, there are many stories of children that play or smear their feces on the wall. Psychologists use that as a symptom that describes Autism; they think it means that the child is mentally unaware, when in actuality the child is putting their finger up there because they cannot easily defecate. As result, they remove their rock hard feces with their fingers. If this painful constipation were resolved, most of these children would not be using their hands.

Often these children then will wipe their dirtied fingers on the bathroom wall or other surface. They don't know how to get this hard, gluey substance off their fingers. To them, the easiest and fastest way is to wipe their fingers on the wall. They don't understand that the best way to clean their hands is to wash their hands with soap and water. Why? Because,

Autistic children have a hard time correlating their present actions with long range benefits. When the parent tells a child to wash his or her hands day to day, the child doesn't see dirt on their hands and doesn't make a connection between washing and cleanliness. Their perception is that they are rinsing clean hands under water. They wash their hands because they are told to, not because they understand that it is cleaning their hands.

A remedy that I have found useful in these situations is mineral oil. You can purchase clear mineral oil from any pharmacy, food store, or convenience store. Give a few drops orally to the young child 1-2 times a week; this is not to be used as a laxative but rather as a lubricant. It coats and lubricates the lining of the intestines just enough to help the particles pass through more easily. At first it is administered 1-2 times a week, but as the child gets better, you should cut back to once a week and eventually once every few months. The important thing is that if you choose to try this old home remedy, that you do so for a *minimum* of 6 months. Otherwise, the gains of the child passing his bowel movements on a regular basis without pain can go away quickly. I have seen some severely autistic kids learn to say, "Can I please have my mineral oil?"

Bear in mind that mineral oil is a petroleum-based product. It is considered safe for internal use according to the Food Standards Agency. Some parents might wish to not use it for this reason and should research alternatives. The author has yet to find anything that works as efficiently and effectively as mineral oil. Remember that the previous instructions say to gradually cut down on the amount used until it is barely needed.

Yeast Issues

What I have discovered working with so many ADHD children is that almost all of them have had a series of infections often beginning when they were little infants. I have been keeping a form on each child, their diagnosis, symptoms and history of illnesses, and on the form I have a question asking whether or not the child had been on antibiotics. Invariably, most had not only been on antibiotics, but many of them had been on between 8-10 different rounds of antibiotics on an ongoing basis. What appears to have happened is that these children have developed Candida from having taken so many antibiotics.

For reducing yeast and Candida, an important step to take includes high doses of acidophilus. While acidophilus is found in some brands of yogurt, it often comes with a lot of sugar, which defeats efforts to remove Candida. A health food store will recommend that you take much higher doses of acidophilus because it puts the healthy bacteria back into the gut that the antibiotics and food additives have destroyed. In my opinion, you would have to eat a truckload of yogurt compared to what the health food stores would provide in a single bottle. There are different kinds of Acidophilus such as Lactobacillus, Primodopholus, and Bifidopholus. I believe that taking different types and rotating them daily is extremely important. Each type seems to work with bowel chemistry a different way and effects how the bowels interact with the rest of the body's organs.

I also feel that it is important to take vitamins and mineral supplements.

The news and media often tell us that vitamins are good for our health, only to come out with another story telling us they are not safe. My personal view is to take large amounts of natural – not *synthetically* made vitamins – and rotate them in the same way you rotate the acidophilus. Of special importance regarding the use of vitamin supplements s is that certain vitamins help some conditions better than others. With special needs kids, vitamins B and B12 should be looked at more closely, followed by Glutathione, vitamin C, and vitamin D3.

A more holistic way of killing yeast it to ingest raw garlic, and if you cannot eat it raw, it may be lightly cooked; make sure it is as close to raw as possible. Garlic has been known for its antifungal properties for centuries. Similar to the effects of detoxification found in Chapter 6, here too, herbs and spices are helpful in combating yeast. Garlic is the strongest of them all, but onion is also quite beneficial. Yeast is living cells. Like all cells, it wants to live and thrive by being in your body. For this reason, I am in favor of taking prescription medication at the start of attempting to kill yeast. As previously mentioned in the book, Oral Nystatin, Oral Sporanox, and Diflucan can help to eradicate yeast overgrowth.

Allergy Issues

For a child who has ADHD, ASD, or seasonal allergies, a simple at-home step to take is to wrap the mattress in plastic. The children affected with yeast tend to have an enormous amount of seasonal allergies, food allergies, recovering ear infections, sinus infections, strep throat, and sometimes urinary tract infections. We are looking to reduce any allergens that make these children ill. They are highly affected by dust mites; they live in carpeting, upholstered furniture, mattresses and pillows. A mattress can literally double in size and grow heavier in less than 10 years; that is because the mattress fills with skin cells and dust mites.

To fix the problem – if you cannot afford a new mattress – is to purchase plastic that goes around the entire mattress and is airtight in order to suffocate the dust mites. Sometimes you can obtain large plastic bags from an appliance store; take several of them for your purpose. You can also purchase one that might zip around the mattress but you must make sure it does not have grommets to let the air in. With some of the younger sicker children who tend to throw-up or wet the bed, it is best to keep the mattress wrapped in plastic for years at a time.

If possible, remove carpeting from the bedroom and have a real wood floor; fake wood floors have a lot of dangerous glues, formaldehyde, and latex-like substances mixed in. Besides, faux-wood laminates scratch and mark-up easily. A throw rug is also suggested, since it can be easily cleaned and washed in a washing machine.

Another thing is to either wash all of any stuffed animals in very hot water (remove plastic eyes to sew back in later), and/or keep them in airtight plastic bags. With one or two being in the bedroom, you must rotate the toys every so often. Be careful of too much frilly curtains around the window and wash these often as well. I know there are children who like to sleep with a down blanket, but a blanket that can be washed often is best. Keep in mind that down can be very allergenic for some. The same rules apply for pillows.

Ear Issues

Prior to the use of antibiotics to stop ear infections, a common remedy was placing garlic oil in the ear; the oil is made for children's ears and is available in health food stores.

Sometimes the garlic oil is mixed with Mullein oil; Mullein oil is an essential oil made from a yellow type of flower. Mullein Oil is regularly used in Europe and Asia. This was one of the old household remedies that were often used in childhood until modern times (Mukherjee, 2012). According to the website Organicfacts.net, there are many benefits to the use of Mullein oil. Mullein oil is known for its use as an analgesic, anti-inflammatory, antiseptic, and even for reducing fevers. It has been said that it is beneficial in treating the ailments of whooping cough, sinusitis, UTIs, and digestive issues. It can eliminate microbial growth. As a disinfectant, it can fight infections in the ear and nose.[xii]

Currently it is popular to use tea tree oil for ear infections; the author recommends you do not use this until you do some research. It has been said that it can disrupt the child's hormonal balance.

There are other ways of dealing with repeated ear infections. It might be worth looking into the art of "candling." Hollow candles for the ears have been around for thousands of years. While you are lying on your side, a hollow candle is placed in the ear with tin foil plate to catch any potential dripping wax. As the hollow candle burns down towards the ear, smoke is produced, melts extra wax and also helps clear the ear. While the candle can be purchased in health food stores, the author urges the parent to use a trained professional rather than experiment with the candles themselves. Care must be taken to see to it that both ears are done properly because if one ear is done more times than the other, it can throw off one's balance. Some senior citizens would benefit greatly from having candling done at the beginning of hearing loss from clogged ears, as it may help to prevent it.

Another major home remedy that I have seen work on countless children is to press down the small flap-like protrusion (known as the Tragus) where the ear meets the face (*not* the earlobe), push it in towards the ear opening, take two fingers with your other hand, place them behind the earlobe slowly under the jaw toward

the middle of your chin with some firm pressure. You are drawing and pulling a little deeply. In effect, you are massaging the Eustachian tube. When this is done properly, what you might find is the fluid or infection that is clogging the middle ear will come out and reach the back of your throat. You will swallow it much like you will swallow phlegm. It might tastes a little salty and you will hear the sound like a toy suction cup being released from a hard surface.

A great time to use this is when your child swims to prevent the swimmer's ear and for people whose ears clog from a shower. I have seen it work on major ear infections, but again, each person is different and you must be sure to check with a medical professional. To learn how to do this for your small child, I recommend you learn how to first do it on yourself; the easiest way is to lie on your back on a hard surface on the floor and follow the steps from the very beginning. When you learn where your own Eustachian tube is, it is easier to locate that of your child's.

Eye and Vision Issues

According to Dr. Akihiro Kawamura – one of Japan's leading brain enhancement researchers and an author of many books relating to the brain and learning process, "The eye-brain connection is only as strong as the eye muscles themselves" (Kawamura, 2007).

Sometimes the eyes are not aligned together properly and do not work in concert with each other for various reasons. Sometimes it is a reflection of internal problems in the body, such as a reaction to vaccines, brain problems, allergies, viral illness (particularly mononucleosis), and toxicity. Even ancient Chinese Traditional Medicine stated that having one of the eyes misaligned was a physical sign of toxicity, linked to problems with the liver or spleen. Both organs deal with the immune system. Nearly all special needs children exhibiting learning disabilities have a condition where the left eye and the right eye do not work perfectly together in tandem. It is as if one eye looks directly forward, but the other eye turns out, up, down or in, and is therefore slightly askew.

While you may not notice this physical misalignment in your child, what you will notice is that most of these children – when doing homework or trying to read a book – lean at their desk or table, extend one arm out and place their face in the crux of that arm; this posture is a telltale slouching or hunched over position. It is not that the children are hunched over because they are lacking motivation or are tired or even lazy. Rather, they are hunched over with their face in their arm in order to block one eye.

When they try to read sitting up with both eyes, they get double vision and the words literally look as if they are moving off of the page. They often skip the next line or words; it is not that these children are aware they are having double vision or blocking one eye, they have almost no knowledge of it. That is because no one ever told them that there is another way to see; this is all that they know and the only way they've ever seen before. I remember when I first went to vision training at the age of 17 or 18 (just before I learned how to read), watching words move off the page and superimpose on to a wall or float in space. I didn't know how I got these words and images to move and I had no idea that everyone else around wasn't doing the same thing. But very quickly in vision training, I became in charge of my eye muscles and of pulling one eye in order to match the vantage point of the other.

Vision training assists with double vision, focusing accommodation, strabismus (when one eye is looking forward and the other is slightly askew), convergence insufficiency (when the eyes don't move toward each other to focus on the same image), and improper binocular vision. Having these conditions means that the eyes are not properly aligned with each other. There are times when an average person may notice such a misalignment. Have you ever found yourself speaking with another adult in conversation who has one eye turned outward and you found yourself not knowing which eye to look at?

Sometimes one will notice a child who wears eyeglasses that always appear to be crooked. Time after time, you take the child to the optician to straighten them out, but the glasses soon become crooked again. The child keeps cocking their head to one side and the glasses get misshapen. This is usually because the eyes, and more specifically the irises, are not symmetrical. For example, one iris might be pointing a little to the right and the other might be straightforward. You may see that one iris is higher up than the other. You may also see the child's head cocked to the left or to the right to compensate. If you try to straighten his or her head out, within a minute he or she will turn his or her head to the one side or the other in an attempt to

straighten out or rebalance the vision. There are a large number of children in schools who have these problems, but of which so easily could be corrected. For all of our neurological, psychiatric, ophthalmological, and sociological fields of study, it is absurd that something as important as vision alignment can be so easily overlooked.

An important feature of vision training is working with convergence, or the ability of the eyes to move and continue to work together as a team, which assists in achieving proper binocular vision. Binocular vision is when both eyes see the same visual target at the same time and how both eyes work together equally and as a coordinated team. If you do not have binocular vision, then you also might not have quality depth perception as well.

Some children become monocular

(read only out of one eye). Sometimes both eyes are open, yet one eye shuts in the brain. An interesting experiment to try to see the effect of one eye shutting in the brain is to stand near a tree or a plant with many small leaves. Close one eye, stare at the plant and then try to touch one of the middle leaves. You'll find it very difficult to get to the desired leaf without first touching the outer leaves. This situation happens because seeing out of only one eye impedes depth perception. It's when your two eyes work together that you can gage how far or how close together something is in space; you cannot do this with only one eye.

According to the website Children-Special-Needs.org, "Many monocular people can be rehabilitated with the help of vision therapy. They can become binocular and gain depth perception."

They claim that there are better results with vision therapy at times than with eye muscle surgery. They go on to describe vision therapy as "physical therapy for the visual system which includes the brain and eyes" (Optometrists Network, 2006). For those interested in researching more on vision issues, there are fancy medical terms for when the eye turns inward, upward, and so on, and also start research with the American Optometric Association.

Another visual condition that contributes to poor binocular vision is Astigmatism (which is blurred vision due to the inability of the optics of the eye to focus a point object into a sharp focused image on the retina). Astigmatism is often fixed with corrective lens.

Nearsightedness, farsightedness, or astigmatism can be corrected with glasses.

But, the problem of having two eyes that do *not* work together is not correctable by the use of eye glasses. Vision training is imperative to correct how the two eyes work together in tandem so that the words do not continue to appear to move off the written page. In my experience, I have never seen special needs kids that did not need at least some vision training type exercises.

Actually going to vision therapy is a lot of fun; it is like going to a gym for the eyes. Sometimes the child is asked to focus on a spinning wheel of colors; focusing on one color while the wheel is moving. Other times images of toys that will move towards the child from close up and then in the distance. As you progress, words and sentences might flash quickly on a screen to get the eyes to look left or right more quickly. Some even have the child jumping on a trampoline or walking on a balance beam to assist the eyes.

I have been showing parents and children alike various eye movements for improving tracking that have profoundly helped these children to later read and write. One common example is when children are continually losing their place on the page of a book and tire of trying to bring their eyes back to the page. A simple at-home exercise that can be performed to correct this situation is one where you hold a pencil about a foot away from the child's face and slowly bring it towards the nose while asking the child to focus his eyes on the pencil, then you bring the pencil back out again slowly. This exercise is repeated over time until the child is eventually able to focus.

A second activity is to bring a vertically held pencil in toward the nose and have the child look at the eraser then over to the wall in the distance past the pencil and finally back again to the close-up eraser. This would be the equivalent of using a close-up lens on a camera and then a panoramic lens.

Another technique is to slowly draw a horizontal figure eight, or an infinity sign, in the air with a pencil while the child follows the tip with his or her eyes. Like the camera lens, the eyes zoom in and out in order to focus from near to far, which these kids cannot perform this task easily. Also, move the pencil at a comfortable distance slowly from the left to the right, watching his or her eyes smoothly tracking together. If one eye moves gracefully but the other eye seems to skip or jump, more needs to be done.

A simple exercise is to take a pen and a pencil and start them off vertically next to each other; make sure the items are about three inches apart. While moving one of the instruments at a time sideways, all out "pen … pencil," "pen … pencil," and make sure to not fall into a pattern that the child can anticipate the next move. Try then, "pencil … pen," "pen … pen," and "pen … pencil" out loud. What you want to do next is to move the pencil further away while saying "pen" or vice versa; there are times you want to trick them with this exercise and their thinking because these special needs children have learned so well how to anticipate what they are going to see, do, and touch, and they almost have a complex of "fear," "then do it." These children have a coping mechanism where they learn how to compensate, but it does not work. This exercise is not about their intelligence, but they will behave as if it is. They will try to prove to you that their eyes can move just fine, when really in actuality they cannot. The point here is to make sure the child does not learn how to anticipate your next move and at the same time to achieve the goal of the child's eyes tracking as one. During these exercises, you do not want the child's head to move but the goal is for them to track the moving items with their eyes and their eyes alone.

All such exercises to have an effect need to be done regularly and for at least 5-10 minutes at a time. These exercises help to improve their sight, perception, reading speed, and comprehension. They also give them back the control that they need. I have found that in these children reading compression is more a function of the ways the eyes are working, rather than the intelligence of the child. In addition to these simple at-home activities there are programs for vision training that you can purchase through an eye doctor. However, these programs tend to be expensive and some of the software can only be used for a limited amount of time.

As simple as some of these exercises are, there are people who just cannot learn until they *learn* how to see. The vision training that I took during my college days in New York City was a true turning point; to this day, nearly all of my students are in need of these exercises and quite frankly, most people would benefit, particularly senior citizens. I feel it is ludicrous that children do not get screened for the need for vision training; it is not included in school systems around the country when they are having academic struggles. It's plausible that vision training can be performed in a resource room or special education department.

Within a few months after beginning vision training, I remember walking down a city street and noticing that the parked cars seemed to get much smaller the further away I was, and as I walked closer to them, they seemed to get bigger. I thought that this was absolutely amazing and wasn't sure what was going on. Before I went to college, I was trying to learn how to draw in perspective and there was a line with a dot, and you were supposed to put something on the imaginary horizon line so that it went back into space, and it was called 3-point perspective. I had little clue as to what this was and it was just dots on a page, a ruler and a bunch of lines. But the day I started to actually see objects appear smaller when they got further away and larger as they got closer, I was shocked. I asked myself "Does everyone see this way? Wow, now I know what they were talking about!"

Sometimes it is always a good idea to find a visual behavioral ophthalmologist *if* you can afford the time and the money, but for those of you who cannot, here is another exercise. Take a thick string or thin rope and put three differently colored beads on it and tie a knot at one end. Then loosely tie the string with the beads to a doorknob and have the child be at eye level with the string while holding it up to their nose; they might have to be squatting on their knees or sitting at a chair, being eye level with the string. You want to move the first bead slowly, inching close to the nose, so that the child will have to look at the first bead and then back to the further away bead; their eyes have to go from close to far away and so on. This will force the lenses in the eyes to change to accommodate the distance. Then, bring in the second bead to the middle of the string so the eyes will go from the closest, to the middle, and the most far away, as they are each in different points in space. So, at a certain point, when the two eyes are working together properly, the string will appear to make the shape of the letter "Y."

I encourage all parents to make the infinity sign with a pen or finger, not only for the vision exercises, but there is knowledge that pertains to rebalancing the left and right hemispheres of the brain. There is something called the midline section; it is in the middle of the horizontal infinity sign where the brain is being asked to shift from one hemisphere from the other.

Your child could easily pick many of these exercises you initiate up and he or she can learn to do them without supervision. Some claim that certain children can read much better with colored lenses. I believe there is some truth to it because I notice once in a great while not only myself but also some of my students seems to read better with yellow lenses. Perhaps it removes glare from the page. This is not an area of expertise, but I have seen it on occasion. When vision training is working and the child is getting better, not only will they read well and skip lines less or lose their place less, they will also appear more coordinated. Take the game of softball for example; the balls come toward the batter and not only do the eyes have to track the balls, but there has to be correct timing for the swing to begin before the ball is in front of the batter. When the two are coordinated, the correct movement of the eyes plus the swing's timing. Some of your children may just be hitting homeruns for the very first time.

Though I have had vision training, while driving at night I will notice that it appears that there are a bunch of cars in my rearview mirror due to the fact that there are headlights behind me. In actuality, it was often just one single car that passed me, so I now know what appeared to be four headlights turned out to be really two headlights. The point here is that I am in control of readjusting and rebalancing my two eyes.

Some people, including doctors, believe that creating eyeglasses with the inclusion of a prism in the glass will help to rotate the eye in lieu of vision training. Despite this way of thinking, my experience thus far has shown that children who are prescribed these glasses will be hesitant and unwilling to wear them.

Instead of using glasses with a prism to help stabilize vision, it is okay to allow and encourage a child to move his or her fingers under the words on a page as they read. This method is frowned upon by third-grade teachers, although some children need to continue to use this method through the upper elementary school grades. Not only learning disabled but some regular children have a drifting eye, so it is necessary for them to use their finger to help them read. It helps keep the eyes on track and flowing from one word or line to the next.

If you are interested in having a child work with an eye doctor specifically trained in the art of vision therapy, my recommendation is that you call the Optometric Center of New York[xiii], tell them where you live, then ask, "Who in my area performs vision therapy?"

Whatever you do, don't go to a regular eye doctor and ask them whether your child needs vision therapy or not; most do not know a thing about it, and the few who do will remark at what a waste of time it is.

I do not fully understand why, but it is my experience that the majority of ophthalmologists are somehow trained in the art of being anti-vision therapy, particularly the eye surgeons. This is very sad because something so simple and noninvasive has the capacity to produce great results.

I recall times when I was hired as a child advocate during mediation procedures and attempting to get the child more services. In this particular situation, this child had been coming to me 1 hour a week for nearly six months. Prior to coming to me, he could hardly read and write and was in the third grade. I had already placed him in vision training with a qualified ophthalmologist and I could tell he was severely dyslexic and took that into consideration during sessions. The child made tremendous progress. Having seen how well he was doing, the parents asked, "Why can't the school do what the tutor is doing?" In this case, the child was already in a special education resource room. The parents tried to work with the child study team on their own, and informed the school that the child was in vision training and in weekly sessions relating to specialized tutoring. Things escalated and a formal child study team and mediation meeting was arranged. The state paid for and *sent* a mediator to the meeting.

At the start of the meeting, I noticed the child study team brought stacks of papers with them. In the very beginning of the meeting after the introduction, the head of the team picked up the papers and started to read. What she was reading were US government reports on how vision training does not help dyslexic students and I was quite surprised. I told her to put the reports away because the child's vision training was just about done. I told her how ludicrous it was that they were spending time and money by bringing in documentation on what does not work with the children in the education system when this child was obviously already substantially better from using it. I then said that they could do all the research they want on the subject how vision training does not help the child, and then I can show research that it does help the child, we'd argue back and forth, and nothing would get resolved. They kept saying vision training does not help

Dyslexia. But the purpose of vision training is not to help with Dyslexia, which was off topic, but to help with the proper physical alignment of the eyes. With the child's reading and writing already jumping up, it was a sad waste of time and energy for the child study team to do biased research rather than focus on what was next for the child.

There are programs you can purchase with discs specifically for vision training. Some vision training eye centers will actually sell you the discs, which I have heard from other clients. Just make sure to find out if the disc you are purchasing has limited single usage (where you can only use it 10 times) or if you can use it indefinitely.

There is a caution when it comes to selecting an ophthalmologist and seeking vision training experts. Unfortunately some are better than others and I have seen many cases where a child might be strung along in program in part because their insurance pays for it; it is was beyond the point of needing more vision training. I have seen other offices turn down a child in great need for vision therapy because it has become too time consuming; a doctor can make much more money making eyeglasses and prescribing them to many people in an hour than spending the time working with one to two children in vision training. Some offices that hold a license hire people to come in and do the vision training for them. These subcontractors can be excellent and some are no good. Regardless of whatever form it takes, working with a struggling student's field of vision can only be a plus and should not be overlooked!

Reading Issues

Phonics, the art of sounding out words, breaking them into syllables, and learning some rules of placement, used to be the basic "normal" approach when teaching reading and writing to young children. Then, one day, specialists from theoretical educational institutions came, bringing new and supposedly "better" methods; whole language and inventive spelling was introduced. Without getting caught-up in details, basically, it introduced the idea that whole words would be best learned on flashcards instead of sounding it out. Children would *memorize* the spelling of the words over and over again.

The Whole Language method may have been okay for the 30% of children who were naturally "visual" learners. However, it was destructive to children who may have been borderline dyslexic or had learning problems. It was also not the best choice for children who learn by listening auditorily, or by touching and feeling, kinesthetically. Not only did it nearly handicap large groups of kids, but also children were permitted to use inventive spelling.

For example, the word "was" was allowed to be spelled "wuz" for several years. As the child grew older, somewhere around third or fourth grade, they would have to then spell words correctly on spelling tests. At this point, the child would have to unlearn the 2-3 years of spelling the word incorrectly and then re-learn the correct spelling. It would be far better to learn the right way from the get-go. I often wonder what the merits were long-term and why so many schools quickly dropped phonics and changed to whole language.

I know that in a whole language classroom young first-graders appeared to be able to read and write; they were told to look at the pictures and figure out what the story was about. So if there was a story depicting a frog and a princess, they would practically know what the story was going to be about based on the pictures alone. However, around third or fourth grade, there are no more pictures in most books. Many of these children that came to rely so heavily on this "prefiguring" were lost. In my opinion, it increased the learning-disabled population.

Thankfully phonics is being reinstated in many schools across the country. The following method is one that should make learning to read extremely easy. I am not sure if I invented it, but I certainly have taken parts of the method to a new extreme. I have been doing this for so many years and no one has yet shown me these same specific methods.

The method begins with using the long vowel-sounding words that usually have a silent "e" at the end, not the short ones that most schools start off with. Words like "bake," "cake," and "take" are good ones to start off with and should be your starting point. The long vowels get a long line (called a 'macron') over them and the silent vowels get a light diagonal slash through it so that you can still see the initial letter. Additionally, the child would be asked to draw an arrow from the silent "e" over to the long "a."

For example, the word "bake" would look like this:

We start with a rhyme. We tell the child "The silent 'e' is the best friend, buddy, to the vowel 'a.' So, the silent 'e' says to his buddy, 'Hey buddy, be long.'" This is a play on the word "belong." Throughout this method, silent letters will continue to get a light diagonal mark through them, which will tell the child not to make the sounds that those letters represent. You want to do as many rhyming words as you can; for instance use "make," "take," and so on.

Often in the very first lesson, you ask the child to come up with his or her own long "a" words. In that first lesson, the child will be asked to write his or her own sentences. They will look up at you because they have never written on their own before; they have only copied from the blackboard. But you, as the instructor, will be making sounds and facial expressions that will support their writing. You might say "the" and you say to the child "You know how to spell 'the;' it is spelled 't-h-e'." Use the phrase "The cake was baked." So I would enunciate, "The c-ay (with my hand up to my ear making an exaggerated long "a" sound)-k- and then silent e (saying "you know what comes what at the end")."

The child must put that macron over the long "a," put the diagonal slash through the "e," draw the arrow from the "e" over to the "a," and has to repeat the implementation of the symbols into the next similar word. The "was" might get a "z" over the "s;" basically, the "s" is pronounced as a "z." I play a game with the use of the period at the end of the sentence. If the child has any learning disability or Dyslexia, the use or the lack thereof of the period will stymie how they

both write and read for years to come.

Now, we are going to handle the long "e." The drill is the same as before. Take the word "tree" for example; we do not pronounce "tr-ee-ee." We only hear the long "e" once. We put the diagonal slash over the last "e," put the macron over the first "e," and the arrow pointing to the last "e" to emphasize "Hey vowel buddy, you be long." Try this with several other words such as the long "I" in "hide" and "ride;" for the long "o," "hope" and "note;" and for the long "u," use words like "blue," "glue," and "use."

Depending on the child and how fast they grasp and retain this information, you can do 1-2 different long vowel words a day. Once they have learned all the long vowels in both reading and writing, you begin the short vowel words, which are inspiring to the learning-disabled child because they are naturally easier. I do it this way, putting the harder words first, because it gives a kind of reprieve to the child. It is almost like a resting point. This is one of the few times that learning to read or write does not get perpetually harder, rather, it gets much easier. This is a really big deal. Seeing a child who runs in the door smiling with an internal feeling that they can do this and it can be fun is quite a precious sight.

Proceeding to the short vowels, they get a small u-symbol above the short vowel sounds as in "a, e, i, o, and u. The sounds will be "a" as in the word "at;" "e" as in the word "egg;" "i" as in the word "it;" "o" as in the word "on;" and "u" as in the word "up." What I like to do is fold the paper in half the long way and put the long vowel team on the left, and the short vowel team at the right. Starting with the long vowel team, put "bake" in the left had column and put "back" in the right hand column. If the word is "take" on the left side, have the child pronounce and write "tack" on the other side with the short team. "meet" goes on the left, and might become "met" on the other side of the paper. "Hide" goes on the left, and "hid" goes on the other side. "Hope" goes on the long vowel team, and it becomes "hop" on the short vowel team. "Blue" goes on the one side, and it becomes "bug" on the right side.

Note: as the child progresses, words like 'night' and 'light' would have the long line above the "i", while the "gh" would have the diagonal line through it. Words like "through" will get a line through the "o," a line through the "g," and the "h" as well. The "u" will get the macron over it. Sometimes it is necessary to put a "t" over the "d" in words like "walked." Then there are other steps in phonics such as teaching the rule of dropping the "e" when adding "-ing." When all of the vowels are learned, I typically do "bake" + "-ing" = baking.

The following image shows an example of what the page should look like higher level books. This allows the early reader to sound out with ease. Some of

with the markings above the vowels, showing the vowel sounds.

bāke	băck
mēet	mĕt
hīde	hĭd
nōte	nŏt
cūte	cŭt

Now here is the part where I have initiated taking this to the extreme. Within approximately ten lessons (5 long vowels and 5 short vowels), the child is now able to read by themselves. I have taken the time to mark-up many chapter books at many levels beginning with early childhood readers then moving on to intermediate books and on to more

you may be wondering if this method will end up handicapping the child. But the trick with the system is that the first few books are heavily marked. As the levels get higher, the markings become less and less, within a few months, there are no markings at all. The child barely notices most of the time. Also, by incorporating writing by the very first day, the child does not become afraid of writing as so many are.

It is best to keep like words in word families, especially in spelling tests. You want to group the long "a" words together, the short "u" words together, and so on. Additionally, after the long and short vowel lessons are completed, individual lessons on digraphs (the "th" sound), followed by the "ch" sound, and eventually the "sh" sound should be done. The order doesn't matter like it does with the short vowels, just as long as you spend several days on each additional lesson.

I think there have been very few children over the years that I could not get them to read and write with this method. Likewise, there have been 1-2 children who became able to sound out words extremely well, read out loud, yet not have a clue what the story meant. They can sound out words and sentences, but have no comprehension of what they just read. I have discovered that some of these children are so highly visual that when a word such as "house" is read, they see a house in their mind's eye. When it comes to words like "the," they don't visualize anything. So a sentence like "The green bug crawled under a bridge and flew by a lamppost" becomes for these kids "green" = green crayon, "bug" = lady bug or bug of choosing, "crawled" = baby crawling, "under" = noting, "bridge" = possibly bridge, "a" = nothing, "flew" and "by" = nothing, and "lamppost" = possibly a lamp. The sentence becomes "Green crayon ladybug baby bridge light." Now you see why they are lacking comprehension. The solution was to create a picture dictionary for some of these non-visual words. An example was the word "the", which I explained as a connection to an object; we drew a line under "the" and "apple" so they would just view it as a connection point. You may need to be creative, but in time you'll find what works for *that* child. It seems that an easy way to do this would be to prefabricate a picture dictionary of prepositions; it may be possible. I think that engaging the child in drawing pictures and using colors keeps a hands-on, kinesthetic, and visual approach together.

The next method I use to help remediate children who are struggling with reading and writing includes a writing game, which encourages creativity and fun with writing. The goal is for the kids to write long descriptive sentences because many children's writing tends to look too simplistic, like this:

I read this book. It was fun. I like this book. You should read this book too.

Many kids that come in my program are almost fearful to write. It appears that they are being taught how ***not*** to write; they are being drilled on not forgetting a capital letter, not forgetting a period, not forgetting a comma, not having a spelling mistake, and so on. Imagine if you were learning how to drive a car and the instructor said, "Don't forget to stop at a stop sign. Don't forget to stop at a red light. Watch out for a dog or cat running into the street. Be sure to watch out for a child running into the street between two parked cars. Check for a yield sign." The details become overly emphasized. It would be focusing more on learning how *not* to drive than learning how *to* drive. You would be so afraid that you would stop and start the car almost every three houses to check for any possible animal, child, and so on that might dart out. This is similar with writing; your children are learning how *not* to write more than learning how to write *properly*.

As I ask them to write, I notice that so many children stare out the window.

Much of their self-talk is, "Oh man, I have to write. Why do I have to write? I don't know what to say!" The following game can hopefully alleviate this. You start the game picking an object to write about; the use of the word "and" is to be extremely limited and should not show up until the game is nearly over. I prefer to use a ball. You, the teacher or parent and tutor begin. Write, "I have a ball," and the student should write at the same time. Then ask the student to add a description. They might write, "I have a red ball." Then you go again, and might add, "I have a red ball with stripes." The child might then add, "I have a red ball with stripes that I got last winter." Then you might add "I have a red ball with stripes that I got last winter during my birthday party." This must continue until the sentence nearly takes up the entire page. What we are looking for is a long detailed fun sentence, but one that is not fragmented and considered a run-on sentence. In practicing this game, we are kind of stretching the mind and the ability to write with a lot of adjectives. The purpose is to inspire the children to naturally write more creatively descriptive sentences on their own when not being tutored.

Another exercise that is loads of fun for children incorporates drawing, writing, sequencing, and test-taking skills. First divide a plain sheet of paper into six boxes so that the child can make a sequential comic strip consisting of two characters. Under each box, draw two lines where the child can write the text. Have the child start by drawing the two characters in the first box, after which make sure every part is colored in with marker once the box is complete. Once that is done, the child has to write two sentences about what is happening in the box. If the box shows a boy and a girl in the woods, the text must simply correlate to what is happening in the drawing.

At all times, once the clothing and colors are established, the characters must wear the same colors throughout the entire strip. For example, if the boy is wearing a green hat in the first box, then he must be wearing a green hat in the last box. This is not a formal "rule" so much as a way for the child to learn continuity and consistency. It helps them to pay attention to detail. By keeping the characters somewhat consistent but changing the setting, background, place, etc., it helps the child get a handle on the idea of sequencing: what comes first, second, last, and so on. After finishing the comic strip

with the six boxes, you then tell the child that they are going to get to write "stupid test questions." By designing the test questions, the child is now using a different part of the brain, switching from pictures to words.

They laugh, smile, and become eager to answer their own questions. I must say, "I'm sorry; you are not allowed to answer the questions, just design the test." In time, they become adept at understanding what is going to be asked and become able to answer the questions on their own without prompting. I have had teachers who are so impressed with a student's work that they actually make copies of the comic strips and hand the test out for the children in the class to answer.

A girl meets a unicorn. She plays with him. Since unicorns are not permitted as pets she hides him. She turns him into just another toy.

What seems to be happening in everyday schooling is that many children sit in class month after month and year after year, always being asked *what* a story was about, *what* the main ideas were, *what* happened, and so on. This is your classic "who/ what/ where/ when/ why/ how," but with many children that could not answer these questions in second grade, third grade, and again in fourth grade, they are not suddenly going to be able to answer them in fifth grade.

The point of having the children write these "stupid test questions" themselves is to develop their ability to independently process information using their own inventive methods. The kids get a fresh perspective by becoming the creative designer of their own test questions instead of being forced to answer typically dull and mundane questions.

Use of Art Therapy

There are many benefits that music and art therapy can offer your special needs child. The child will advance visually, conceptually, and physically with hand to eye coordination and long-term cognitive thinking. Any artistic activity – whether it is a drawing with pencil, crayons, or a painting – will develop hand to eye and cognitive skills as long as the entire page or canvas is filled-in. This includes the background.

The more time a child spends completing a picture, the better the results.

One of the typical problems when it comes to art concerning special needs kids is that they will scribble a little picture in the middle of the page, and then say they are done. They'll say "I'm finished. I drew it. I'm done!" By getting them to add more thought to the empty space, the most progress can be made developmentally. It doesn't matter if the child's drawing is good or not, we are looking at the quantity on the page, not quality at this point. If you get the child to fill up the entire page on a regular basis, you will notice a lot of areas in their life start to improve; they overlap.

For now, let's get right to some details! In this first exercise, you will need a regular store-bought palette of water colors and a new paint brush that comes to a fine point. I find that the Chinese brushes made of bamboo work particularly well.

You should get the kind of brush that the hairs don't come out while painting. You will also need a pad of water color paper from a craft store; this is not the same thing as saying the pad can be used for drawing as well as water colors.

In this exercise have the child paint tiny dots of different colors using watercolor paints and a pointy brush. Since they are not painting a picture of "something," there should be no judgements. The dots must be close

The reason you specifically want a watercolor pad is because it is thick, almost like a cardboard, and it won't rip and buckle when used properly. Though you are using an inexpensive paint set with basic colors, I have chosen these materials because they are somewhat clean and hardly any preparation or clean-up is necessary. You pre-wet some of the colors with one drop of water on the cakes and the child will put the point of the brush into the water droplet and paint mixture until there is a nice amount of paint on the brush itself. You will have them paint tiny little dots very close together; the smaller the dot and the closer together, the better the exercise.

Let's say you start with the color orange; afterwards you rinse the hairs with the orange in it, and then you go right into the color red and continue dot painting in any direction. Repeat this with all the colors; limit it to 4-5 color choices. The child is encouraged to go in any direction to fill the page, but make sure there are white spaces in between groups of dots. The painting should not be representative of any one particular object. When the whole page has been completed, the project is finished.

This project sounds so simple, but let's take a look at what's being accomplished. First of all, the child is learning to control the tool. Secondly, the child has to give some kind of focused thought throughout the page. Next, they are freed up from worrying about what it will look like, whether it's good or bad, or from any judgment whatsoever. It is often a calming and almost meditative exercise. Many children will begin to innately *want* to continue to draw and paint from this one little exercise. It is recommended that you the parent or a caregiver also paint your own picture alongside the child's using the same dot method.

Another great artistic pursuit is having your special needs child develop an interest in photography. Your cell phone is a great place to start. Just let the child take photos at random and practice composing the shots.

Sleep Issues

After examining many special needs issues concerning the body, this final section of this chapter looks at sleep issues, which can be very frustrating to most parents. Much of the time, children with Autism and ADHD have significant trouble falling or staying asleep. You want them to go through all the different stages of the sleep cycle. All the stages of the sleep cycle are necessary to maintain total health and well being. After first checking with your medical practitioner, you may find that melatonin will help your child fall asleep and stay asleep. Melatonin is something that is provided in the natural rhythm of light and dark.

Before the advent of electricity, we went to sleep as the sun set and woke up as the sun rose. In today's world, we've fallen out of that pattern. While in times past the body would have produced melatonin more readily, in today's natural night and day cycles we are less able to generate this chemical naturally to help us fall asleep. Melatonin can be purchased in food and health stores over the counter for as little as 5 dollars, and is usually found in the vitamin section and is readily available at your local supermarket. It is amazing how a little melatonin can change your child's sleep patterns.

Other tips for sleep inducement include removing electronic devices and lamps. The use of night lights also disrupts the production of melatonin. The body needs total darkness for effective melatonin production. While everyone knows it's best to shut the television and the lights off, my point of view is that if your child can only fall asleep with the TV being on in their bedroom then let them have it. If possible, try to get a timer that shuts off the device an hour or two after they go to their room. Make sure all electronic devices are as far away from the child's bed because they emit electromagnetic radiation at all times. For this, the less exposure, the better; this also goes for adults. I am not a purist, but I have my TV as far away from my head as possible in my bedroom as well.

I have given you a plethora of directions and somehow feel like I have just breezed through but I am asking the reader to thoroughly invest time with each of the aforementioned exercises and remedies. If I had the privilege of working with your child, I would be spending months on each. Don't gloss over them; take it more seriously. Parents should instinctively find out what remedies work best and stick to them in the long run.

Chapter 8: Early Interventions: Reorganize, Reassign, Relearn

The previously mentioned methods of detoxifying, such as taking vitamins and minerals, eating raw organic foods, soaking in mineral baths, and sweating out toxins, should produce good healthy results. These methods are good for both your special needs child and for you as well. Now you are *ready* to be exposed to the importance of early intervention.

Plasticity of the Brain

The brain is at its fastest-growing and most flexible point from the ages of birth to approximately nine or ten-years-old. There are many studies that prove that the development of language is more or less a prime aspect of the brain – from birth to approximately age three. It is a pivotal time when children learn language and are talking. You can expose a child at this age to several languages and they will pick them up with ease. Try to expose an adult, however and it will be much more difficult for them to grasp and fluently speak a different language.

Imagine if you will that the structure of the brain is similar to that of a tree. The trunk would represent the brain stem. The branches that get smaller at the top of the tree would be similar to the veins/arteries and neurons. Using the analogy of the tree, if one part is damaged, the other part risks death or disease as well. If you do not help the damaged part of the tree, the other part might be vulnerable to wood-boring insects, fungal infection, and decay. If however a good Arboretist comes along and takes care of the damaged part of the tree through pruning and providing nutrients, the tree has the capacity to regrow. That is what I'm asking you to do with the brain-damaged child. In essence, I'm asking for intensive therapies that can "reboot" the brain, and "re-grow" the parts that were damaged. Once the tree is healthy, the branches continue to grow and there is a myriad of new branches, and new pathways.

A healthy, robust tree rebalances itself; if a major limb is damaged, the tree simply grows a new one. When a healthy tree comes into its season, a fantastic array of leaves and blooms occur; that is the potential outcome for your child. An extreme example of a brain's ability to re-grow can be found in severe epilepsy where the seizures are life-threatening, and it is determined that parts of the brain must be removed. Amazingly, after some early

intensive therapies and rehabilitation, the brain can sometimes re-grow its functions in the remaining areas.

A Hemispherectomy is the removal of as much as half the brain. "The Hemispherectomy performed today involves both resection and disconnection of pathways along which seizures travel. The procedure is effective because of the unique ability of a young child's brain to re-organize, reassign important functions, and re-learn tasks. This ability is known as plasticity" (Weill Cornell Medical College).

Also, some stroke victims with the inability to walk, talk, or carry on daily activities can in fact relearn their skills with intensive therapy, using a different part of their brain. The period in which they can relearn is immediately after the stroke because there is a limited window of opportunity to 'reboot' the brain. Much in the same way that a stroke victim relearns, so too can your autistic child, provided that it is done early.

To reiterate, the brain is able to re-grow'; it can reorganize, reassign, and relearn. If the brain has the capacity to physically re-grow after an operation where half of it is removed, then it can surely have the capacity to re-grow its functions in your child.

There is a window of opportunity from birth to approximately the age of 10 where this can be done quickly and effectively. According to a recent study published in the *Journal of Autism and Developmental Disorders* by Yale Child Study Center researchers Dr. Fred Volkmar, Kevin A. Pelphrey, and their colleagues, "When given early treatment, children with Autism Spectrum Disorders (ASD) made significant improvements in behavior, communication, and most strikingly, brain function, Yale School of Medicine researchers report in a new study." If a child has not received the intervention of therapy when young during this dynamic time, then dramatic recovery is not likely to take place (Association for Psychological Science, 2011). They can get better, but might not fully come out of Autism. The earlier they receive therapy, the better the results.

These interventions allow for the window to stay open past the age of 10. Every moment is to be a therapeutic moment; there is no time for rest. I personally have seen fifteen and sixteen year-olds make dramatic improvements because their windows were still open. It is up to *you* to effectively keep that window open for as long as possible.

Speech, Physical Therapy, and Occupational Therapy are essential; so are music and art therapies. Different functions come from different parts of the brain.

It does not matter much in my opinion how certified the instructor is; what matters is the connection between the therapist and the child. What matters most is that the child is drawn to and *trusts* the person providing therapeutic services. A young college student can become as effective as a trained therapist. A grandfather also can reach a child. It need not be about spending large sums of money. A parent can spend a fortune getting a specifically trained therapist and see little outcome, but barter with another mother and receive great results. An example is ABA Therapy, which stands for Applied Behavioral Analysis Therapy,

which uses a lot of rewards and punishments towards having the child behave a certain way. I've seen people using just the idea of play therapy get similar or even better outcomes. ABA is considered the "gold standard," but is not always necessary; it has a lot of fancy names and credentials, but it's nothing new.

ABA built itself up to be accepted by medical insurance companies. For a number of our kids, it also seems to be beneficial, but other children have gone through ABA and have come out sounding like robots; the takeaway here is that once again, not all therapy is for all children. As a parent, you must scrutinize the benefits in your child every few months. The point is that all of these therapies are generally expensive. Some are not covered by insurance. An overwhelmed parent can compensate without spending tons of money. Do not feel guilty if you cannot afford the current trends. I ask that the parents *trust their instincts.*

Various Types of Therapy

Physical therapy focuses on gross motor skills, e.g., walking, jumping, hopping, running; while occupational therapy focuses on fine motor skills such as holding a pen, cutting with scissors, buttoning buttons, opening and closing zippers and snaps. Physical therapy includes having the child formulate where they are in space: not only can I walk to the door, but also can I do so without crashing into an object? Special needs children can confuse ideas such as distance, timing, and balance. How they place their body on the chair can also be an issue. Take for example the act of a person walking. To most it is an automatic process, but to a child affected with Autism, Hypotonia, or Dyspraxia, in which certain muscles are strong while others are weak, there is nothing automatic about this process at all. Walking includes moving the heel and toe, bending of the knees, and flexibility that these children can have problems with. Many times I have seen autistic children toe walk or stretch their legs so rigidly that they have locked their knees and appear to walk like toy soldiers. It is as if there is a disconnect between the muscles and the limbs. These children tend to fall forward a lot; some fall off their chairs when in a sitting position. At times their heads are down just so they can see the ground. Proper walking, sitting, running, and hopping can take years of therapy.

In order to have you feel what it would be like for a child who cannot walk properly, imagine putting a 300lb weight on your right leg, a 50lb weight on your left leg, a 200lb weight on your right arm, and nothing on your left arm. Now I ask you to coordinate the muscles on each limb and walk easily across the street; you would have to stop and relearn how much force and agility each limb required. Likewise, with careful observation, you can almost tell when a child is autistic by observing them. This situation doesn't necessarily relate to children with Asperger's, but in Autism; there's a certain lack of elasticity in these children's movements that can be somewhat choppy and jerky. Sometimes their hands seem to shake, almost as if they have mild Parkinson's disease. They are clumsy and sometimes one leg moves back and forth,

as well stiffen if they are waiting on a line. Their movements are inconsistent, sometimes barely noticeable to others and their movements are more profound.

A good occupational therapist works with areas that include assertiveness, cognition, or independent living for the older child. They also work with community resources, home management, medication management, time management, and safety in the home and in the community.

Speech therapy is the art of remediating problems making sounds, pronunciation, stuttering, and putting words together, as well as understanding language through the use of oral exercises such as tongue, lip, and jaw.

Art therapy is a relatively new field and is sometimes a form of psychotherapy that uses art media. It develops another form of communication. Art itself has been around since the beginning of time and can be done at home or in playgroups. Getting children to manipulate sand, clay, paint and paintbrushes with joy and freedom is beneficial. While there indeed is the American Art Therapy Association that sometimes stresses psychotherapy through art, Mandalas, painting, drawing, cartooning, or even creating crafts, they can elicit a certain calming effect while opening the mind to new creativity. Doing simple activities like these allows for opportunities for the child to escape from their difficulties. Getting children to become spontaneous with art or music and taking initiative helps them get well. Getting a child who seems to be lost in his or her own world, redirecting them into art and creativity can inspire a give and take type of relationship with other people, leading towards other people and their surroundings. Giving children art supplies can give them a sense of control over their environment.

Music therapy is particularly meaningful. Nearly all people relate to music in a natural way. You may see your special needs child rocking to it, smiling, or tapping, making a drumbeat sort of noise. It is interesting to learn that from birth to approximately age four, music and math use the same part of the brain. It is as if math and music are from the same branch of the tree. As the child gets older, the branch splits to one side becoming math and the other becoming music. It is interesting that many doctors say that they had to make a choice between music and medical school and many doctors were actually very musical at some point in their lives. Some musicians say that they had to make the same choice as well. Music therapy does not necessarily mean playing a particular instrument. To an infant, shaking a rattle, bouncing a ball, running with a free-flowing scarf to music, some benefit will be gleaned. Music therapy works best in groups, as withdrawn children can watch others around them move to the music. Music therapy is active. Not just sitting and listening to music but taking an active role. Programs such as Music Together and Kinder Music are available throughout the country. By exposing your infant to music you are unknowingly exposing them to math as well.

Water therapy can help the child have a body-mind connection. Floating, playing in the water, and the overall feeling of weightlessness, can be incorporated towards creating health.

Often children have a sensory overload, thus when you touch them slightly, they might feel as if they are being hit with great force. On a cold day they can feel hot, on a hot day they can feel cold. Again there seems to be a disconnect between their senses and surroundings. Sometimes their senses are way under developed and they feel very little. Water therapy can help such children adjust better.

Sensory Integration therapy is very similar to play therapy in that they use activities such as crawling in a tunnel, playing under a parachute, or balancing on a beam in an effort to play while focusing on different senses. Some ADHD and autistic kids spend a lot of time alone and playing does not come natural to them. It is a skill that can be taught and learned. Often, they can become aggressive or cry if they don't win in a board game or race.

Some of these kids believe that the reason the other person won was to hurt them, and not because they enjoyed the game. Reciprocity is particularly difficult as they must follow guidelines, listen to the other person, and be able to give and take. It is particularly hard for some ADHD or autistic children to empathize with another. Special needs children exposed to common activities such as those in Gymboree receive invaluable benefits but for children having difficulties it can be even more valuable in the long term.

Behavior modification

Behavior modification is a simple system that strives to reward children for good behavior. If the child has bad behavior, you would to attempt to structure good behavior. There are a lot of theories on behavior modification using a system of rewards for good behavior and ignoring the behaviors in an effort to *not* reinforce bad behaviors, but if a child begins to become dangerous to themselves or others, then behavior modification can be too little, too late.

In this method, you first define a problem: *does not wash hands after the bathroom.* For very ill children with disruptive behaviors, you want to select a positive reinforcement and give it to them often. For example, if your child responds well to a food or a snack, such as a piece of chocolate, the child would receive the chocolate for good behaviors. In the beginning, it would be frequent and often. Let's say you want the child to start putting away his or her toys and crafts each time they are used; in this case, pleading, asking, and reminding the child won't work. Initially, you can reward the child with candy every single time they clean after themselves. In a few weeks, they might need to clean up three times in a day before earning the candy. Eventually, they might need to clean up for five days in the week before earning the chocolate. It can be the same with small toys. Also, a child may earn a sports card or anything else that the child likes, instead of candy, for example.

You want to apply the reinforcement consistently to change or shape the behavior. Some parents may worry that the child would get fat from all that candy or even become dependent on earning rewards for good behavior. That is not the case because as a child improves, the rewards are spaced out further and further apart. What originally took a day might take a week or a month to earn now.

The best part of the program is that when it is done well, the child learns to reward him or herself. The child will tell him/herself, "You did a good job," or even a mere smile becomes the reward for said simple action.

The other thing I love about behavior modification is that it can reduce the pattern of yelling and pleading that parents often fall into. An example is, if your son or daughter promises to do his or her homework after a snack and then manipulates it to being after a TV show and a snack. The parent becomes exhausted with the constant changes. If the parents reward for doing homework *before* the snack, there will be no argument, and the parent will not need to renegotiate the terms.

With a young child, it is a good idea to have every task charted on the refrigerator. As they age, charts will not be necessary. Please note that this is not a static system; it is to bend and change with the child and when it works properly, it will no longer be needed.

In an article I wrote in 2009, published on the Home EDucators Resource Directory, entitled *"How to Prevent Urgent Meltdowns,"* I go into great detail on behavior modification:

"Question: My child's 'meltdowns' have become more explosive and embarrassing both in private and in public as he/she has gotten older. I have tried using various methods; I have used behavior modification such as stickers, rewards, and charts, but it does not work. Can you help me with this growing problem? Answer: Using behavior modification techniques are fine, until more action is necessary. Upon reaching this point, another method is called for. At this time, all the stickers and rewards in the world would not calm the child/teen down. A more immediate solution can ease the situation.

In the book, *The Explosive Child,* by Ross W. Greene, the basket A, B, C system is mentioned. To make it simple, basket C is when the child erupts with whining, crying, yelling, and using awful behaviors, but not harming others. Basket B represents more aggressive behaviors, and the child might throw objects. Basket A becomes violent and may develop into a life threatening situation because the child might injure himself or others, might run into a busy street, or knock someone down.

My experiences with these types of children have enabled me to help other parents learn what kinds of physical symptoms and behaviors lead up to basket C. You want to become aware of what your child does preceding the basket C level. You might notice the child's breathing changes (they might grunt). They may flex their muscles. Their arms, hands, and legs might become rigid. You might see their face or ears turning red. Some kids will say that they have stomachaches and headaches, and not just to get your attention. They are communicating their pain/ anger indicating an oncoming flair-up. Do not ignore these indicators with an explosive child, even though some behaviorists and experts say to disregard these signals (Wakefield, 2010). For your already explosive child, it is simply too late.

What you must do is, according to Dr. Greene, "do whatever it takes to prevent the initial basket C behaviors" (Greene, 1998). Simply trying to pressure the already melting-down child may cause a negative reaction. I am not asking you to simply give in to what the child wants at all times: however, I am asking you to acknowledge what sets your child off in order to prevent them from entering into the basket C behaviors.

This method is directed at the explosive, somewhat older, child who might have ADD/ADHD or be on the Autistic Spectrum Disorder, and any other severe and atypical children. Obviously this is not the correct approach when teaching a typical toddler or small child. Just giving in to a small child's wishes and cries is not in their or your best interest.

There are various government run programs for emergencies in all states in which a parent can call for help and a van can be dispatched to the home within 12 hours of the call. The purpose of the van is to bring therapists to help defuse the situation, enabling the family to stay intact. Otherwise some of these kids can end up in treatment centers or locked up. In New Jersey, there is

one program called the SMILES program and another by the name of C.I.F.A.

You might find yourself in a grocery store at a checkout line by the register. Just as you're unloading the groceries, your child becomes so disruptive that you can hear the whispers of the other adults around you. Their judgments that you're spoiling the child or that he/she needs a spanking is void of the knowledge that your child might have a medical condition. While it is humiliating, you feel like turning around and apologizing to them, however, your child is getting worse by the moment. At this critical time, you could ask the store manager to put the entire shopping cart into the refrigerator and take the child home. The manager should understand that you might return later that day without the child to pay for your purchases. Simply trying to hurry up and pay at the register may worsen your child from basket C to basket B, and even basket A.

What I am asking you to do is say to yourself, "Is what I am doing working, should I remove him or her from the environment, should I be taking him or her home, and at the home should I take my child for a walk outside?" In time, you will relearn how to look over your shoulder and take notice of your child's physical, emotional, and psychological affects. Once you learn how to defuse your child before he/she erupts, a lot of hope and positive results lay on the road just ahead. Your child will then make progress, whether at home, in school, or camp.

Eventually your explosive child will calm down and get benefits by using the more moderate forms of behavior modifications and rewards. The point of the basket system or behavior modification is to eventually have the children innately regulate themselves without needing an external system. One violent ASD child, by age 11, would run into his/her room and shut the door without having to be told that he or she was punished. Fifteen minutes later the child would open the door and ask, "Is my punishment over now?" And that, my dear reader, would bring a smile to any parent's face."

Similarly, another example may be if you are driving somewhere and your explosive child starts to whine and cry; he/she then acts out by kicking the driver's seat or throwing objects towards the dashboard. It is time to pull the car to the side of the road or to a nearby parking lot. Do not continue to drive. Do not think,

"Oh we'll get to our destination in 10 minutes." Stop the car and let the child know that you will remain there until their disruptive behavior stops. It doesn't matter if you are on the way to school, a doctor's appointment, or a movie. The most important thing is that you don't let behaviors escalate from "C" to "B" to "A," as previously explained. Consistency is vital. When the child figures out that you will *always* stop the car with disruptive behavior, in a short time, they will learn that the car is no place for a meltdown. In fact, once the child learns never to have a meltdown in the car, on rare occasion, you might end up taking the child who is having a meltdown in the house to the car for a short drive to de-escalate the situation.

An extremely useful tool to have in your wallet or on your person at all times is a note printed as a business card that says, "My child has a medical condition. If he or she behaves inappropriately, there is a medical reason." I have found that trying to explain the behavior of a disruptive child to onlookers is a difficult and uncomfortable thing to do. Onlookers may be thinking "What a spoiled brat!" By turning around and handing them the card, they immediately soften and sometimes, even may try to help. Responses such as "Oh my nephew has this," or "My grandchild gets this way too" turns a crisis into an empathetic moment.

This is a good time to hand out the card explaining your child's unusual behavior. Generally bystanders will warm up and assist you once they have read the card.

Chapter 9: Special Education Services

Do not delay the seeking of therapeutic or professional help because of other people's opinions. If your instincts say something is wrong then jump into intervention right away because there is no harm in doing too much; the only harm is not doing enough. It is sad for me to hear that a parent got a call from a school's child study team when their son or daughter was near the end of second grade, requesting an evaluation.

Usually, child study team evaluations can take up to six months to complete; meanwhile the child is losing precious time. If Autism is considered, it may turn out to be too little, too late. On the bright side, much can still be done. It is just that, had intensive therapies begun earlier, the radical improvements might have taken a faster pace. The window may have begun to close slightly, but it is not yet shut!

If the Child Study Team determines that your child is eligible for special education services, then a formal "Individual Educational Plan" (IEP), will be constructed. It is surprising how many services can be provided and paid for by your local school district. Most families do not find this information out until it is way too late. For one, parents tend to believe the schools when they say that they have their children's best interests at heart, but like most things in today's economy, schools do not do one step more than what they have to do. Services are cut all the time because of budget cuts and financial problems. It is up to the savvy parent to do their own research or hire an advocate/tutor that can help them navigate the system. For example, the school might determine that your child is eligible under the IEP for speech therapy. The school schedules one time a week with a group of other children. BUT, your child really needs one on one therapy two or three times a week. You are actually entitled to request this one on one individual therapy but if you do not know that you can do this, you will not have the best services for your child. Most parents believe that the schools are giving them an optimum amount of service, but in actuality they are giving them the bare minimum. Know the laws.

Parents should know that there are certain basic therapies that your child is entitled to under *the Individuals with Disabilities Education Act* (IDEA), which is a federal law enacted in 1990, reauthorized in 2004. It is designed to protect the rights of students with disabilities by ensuring that all children with special needs receive a *free appropriate public education* (FAPE), regardless of ability. Furthermore, IDEA strives not only to grant equal access to students with disabilities but also to provide additional special educational services and PROCEDURAL SAFEGUARDS (National Resource Center on AD/HD, 2011). The National Resource Center on ADHD goes on to state "Special educational services are individualized to meet the unique needs of students with disabilities and are provided in the least restrictive environment" (2011).

Getting Proper Services for Your Child

So let's say your child has a

learning disability, is struggling with reading and writing, might be dyslexic, and hates school, what should you do? Step one is to ask for a formal child study team evaluation to see if your child is eligible for services under special education. If the child study team says that your child is not eligible based on their testing, then you can require them to pay for outside experts to come in and test your child, as it is part of the child study team requirements. If after having your child assessed with outside experts still does not help you obtain services, then you could follow the law of the land and start a "due process hearing."

Every school must provide a parent with the *"Know Your Rights in Special Education"* booklet yearly. This booklet is not to be taken for granted or taken lightly. It gives step-by-step instructions on how

to proceed with a Child Study Team. If you follow it precisely, the odds are that you will win your case without having to step foot into a "due process hearing." You will not even need a lawyer to help you through this. Sadly, often special education lawyers are not known for winning these cases anyway.

I am now going to highlight some of the essential steps to take when seeking to get services for your child that can save you a lot of wasted time and agony. Many parents often receive verbal promises from the teacher or a school administrator that their child will be helped or paid attention to more, only to find that, though they were well-intentioned, no action was taken. In the booklet, it states that everything should be in writing so there is no confusion as to what takes place with your child. Not only should everything be in writing, but multiple copies should be sent to a variety of people. All copies should be then sent to the superintendant of the district, the principal of the school, the head of the Child Study Team, and to the teacher. You might be amazed at the different kinds of responses you get once the superintendent of the district is informed. Much of the time, when verbal promises are made, and the parent files for any kind of "due process hearing," the district will claim that the superintendant did not know anything about the situation. It is like having a trump card played against you. There are specific amounts of days after a parent makes a request, preferably written, in which the school must comply. In the event that they do not comply, the parent would win the "due process hearing." The author would like the reader to know that there are some districts that would be more than happy to accommodate your child's needs from the day the letter is written, they are ready to service you and your child and team up with you immediately. For unknown reasons, there are some schools on the other hand that will fight you to almost never give services. The best thing to do is assume that the school is there to help you and take the path of least resistance.

After the evaluation has been done, the results are discussed from all the testing. If the child meets the criteria, then an Individual Educational Plan (IEP) is formerly constructed, delineating the goals and objectives for the particular child. All accommodations are written out, such as whether or not your child is going to receive individual aid, untimed tests, what therapy is to be used and its frequency, whether or not your child needs adaptive gym, the scheduling, whether homework is to be modified, whether the child can use a laptop computer rather than handwritten notes, whether the child has behavior management place, and whatever else is appropriate.

Individual Educational Plans

The Individualized Education Plan (IEP) is the cornerstone of a student's educational program. A child study team, or a group of people that meet in order to assess a child's educational needs, creates this plan after an assessment. Every school has a child study team. Unfortunately, a lot of the money goes into the team *"studying"* the child. A lot of money is spent for a neurologist, a behaviorist, and a psychiatrist. It seems that more money goes towards *studying* the child rather than providing vital services. After the child is

assessed as having a neurological, emotional, intellectual disability, having ADHD, Dyslexia, is on the spectrum, an IEP or individual educational plan is put in place.

It is a document that is signed by members of the study team and the parent that defines what is to be done during a school day. "The child is to receive extra help during math. The child is to receive speech therapy two times a week." It outlines different methods to help the child to achieve. It documents things like, "Johnny will spell words accurately 80% of the time at the second grade level. Johnny will be able to read a paragraph with 80% comprehension." In its inception, it was a well-intended document; the goals and activities were clearly spelled out.

An IEP meeting has a formal structure; it includes the head of the child study team, a learning disabilities professional, in some cases the principal, and a social worker or school psychologist. If your child is found eligible for special education services and an IEP is created, you will be informed that the IEP must be redone every three years. But often what you are not told is that you have the right to have as many IEP meetings as you want. It is not necessary to wait three years for the meeting; in fact, make sure you do not wait that long for follow up meetings. While you do get a yearly meeting to go over new goals and placement for the following year, it is not the same as a complete re-evaluation.

Three years is an awfully long time to wait to improve the outcome for your child's education. For example, in the very early years when a child first learns how to write – sometimes as early as kindergarten – they are often taught to write using capital letters only. Then a year or two later, they are re-taught to use a capital at the beginning of a sentence and small letters for the rest of the sentence, unless when it comes to a proper noun. Many of the Dyslexic, Autistic, and ADHD children will have a terrible time re-learning, and some will never make that transition. In this case, waiting until third grade to help the child accommodate for their difficult writing is far too long. It would be far better to put in a child's IEP that when it comes time for a child to learn how to write, they learn to use initial capital letters from the very first day; make sure they only learn the right way and do not switch styles.

Furthermore, most children are exposed to the "ABC song," but for some challenged children it is not usually a benefit to learn it. Take for example the letter "C;" in some words it has a harsh sound as in the work "CAKE," in other words it has a soft sound as in the "CENTS." If you think of the song for a moment, it sounds like a "SEE" pronunciation; it will do more harm than good in the long run. Even worse would be isolating the letter "E," as in "EAGLE," "EGG," completely silent in many other words, and sometimes like an "I," as in the word "RECEIVE." So the song would have to sound something like this: "A/AH, B, C/KA, D, E/EH, I, FAH, GAH, H," and so on … have I confused you enough? This might apply to many learning disabled children. Thus, it is important that the IEP specifies in writing how the child

is to be taught in a manner that best benefits their learning style.

So, great time and effort is taken to arrange for all these people to meet with the parents. After advocating for children for more than 25-years, I have come to learn of a 'trick' that many schools play on unsuspecting parents. What I noticed is that many schools would place a phone call to the parents from a day up to a week before the meeting to announce that one of the school personnel could not make the IEP meeting and ask if you want to go ahead with meeting anyway. While it may appear that it is not a big deal that one person doesn't show up, in actuality, it's a huge deal. If the parents do not agree with the outcome of the meeting and want to have either a "due process hearing" or a state mediator assist, the school will then inform the parent an IEP meeting never occurred because that one specific personnel … "Mr. So and So," was not in attendance. During my time as a paid advocate - the first five or so times that I have seen this situation occur in the different schools and districts - it seemed that it was just unplanned happenstance. After awhile, when a majority of schools in different areas continually did this, I came to the point where I had to prepare the parents in advance to deal with such a response.

There were times when the parent received a call from the school that "Mr. So and so" could not make it and the parents would then put the school on hold, calling me up asking if they were sure they were supposed to postpone the meeting. I have come to use this scenario as a sort of litmus test in which, if the school does this, I know they are only in favor of the administration. If they do not do this, they are most likely in favor of meeting the best needs of the child. I suppose there are exceptions; I just haven't seen many of them in the past two decades. It is always best to prevent the need for a "due process hearing" and try to maintain an air of friendliness with the school. I have seen schools change test scores in order to win these cases; the reason being that many of these schools have adopted inclusion in education.

IEPs are are supposed to be written for your individual child; many are not. More and more school districts now have pre-written IEPs. In the past ten years, perhaps because of the consolidation of resources, they have written these goals and objectives onto a template and created IEP A and IEP B, so when a new child enters the school they can press a button to put the child's name on it. In fact, you can pretty much change the name on the IEP and not be able to tell the difference. They are entirely generic and benefit the school, but have little or no benefit for the individual child. If your school does this, do not permit it.

Instead, a *properly* written IEP would be specific and state the child's progress and goals. An example of a well-written IEP statement would be, "Johnny is at the 2.3 level in mathematics and by June we hope to see him at the 3.3 level." In other words, Johnny is performing at the second grade, third month level and by June, we should see him at the third grade, third month level.

The problem is, while the goals are to be written on the document and methods of obtaining those goals are to be clearly spelled out, there is no real way to tell if the child met the goals. Sentences like "Johnny will get better at math," and "Johnny will receive extra help in math 2-3-times a week," leaves it up to the teacher's opinion whether Johnny improved or not. If you as a parent are not satisfied with Johnny's math progress, who can you go to, to prove that the goal was not met? After all, Johnny did receive extra help in math 3-times a week and his math supposedly did improve.

The point here is that the goals must have tangible, measurable results. A more appropriate way for the IEP to identify that Johnny is at a 2.3 level in math while in the third grade. In June, we anticipate him being at a 3.3 level. This means that at the beginning of third grade, Johnny's math ability is equivalent to a second grader in the third month of the school year and the IEP is looking to see that Johnny makes a full year's improvement, thereby ending at a third grade level the third month, by the time he's ready to enter fourth grade. He is still behind, but it showed that he made a year's worth of progress. That would be a very good result. In this scenario, if Johnny ends up still at a 2.3 level at the end of third grade, more accommodations are necessary. If Johnny were performing similarly to this in other subject areas such as reading and writing, this would be the time to call for another IEP meeting. If Johnny were sitting at the back of the classroom with an aid in the so called "inclusion" program, he most certainly needs to be pulled out from the inclusion and go to a more restrictive environment, but with one-on-one or small group instruction in a resource room and/or an all day multiple disabilities class. Do not be afraid of the word "restrictive;" I know it sounds punitive, but all it means is an increase of services in a smaller program. By law, this would call for a change in the IEP.

The law surrounding the IEP is clear: they must be reviewed and rewritten every three years. If a fourth grader is struggling, waiting until seventh grade to reassess is wasting a lot of time! Most parents do not realize that it is in their right to demand a reevaluation with new goals as often as they like and it is their do diligence to have this happen. If you find that the child is not making the type of progress that he or she could and should then call for an IEP meeting every six months. You are permitted to have your child studied by someone out of the district as well.

It is imperative that you have your child evaluated by someone that understands the system. The way it stands now, the evaluation is often a teacher's opinion rather than measurable levels. The advocator can be someone as close as a neighbor or as official as a social worker. All families in which a child is eligible for special education must be given a *"Know Your Rights in Special Education Handbook."* This book along with the IEP is the most important documents you have. In the event that you are not satisfied with the child's progress and how the IEP is administered, my advice is that you read and follow the step-by-step procedure in this handbook.

The procedures specify how many days it can take for a school to remedy the situation. Parents often spend years being told by the teacher or promised by the child study team to help the child. The handbook specifies that all communication be in writing with multiple copies. Don't forget that if there is a grievance, it is important that the superintendent of the district be informed in writing. Parents have spent years listening to teachers or members of the child study team or chatting during phone calls only to find out that the program did not follow the IEP. As stated previously in this chapter, not only must the superintendent of the district receive a copy of the letter, but so should the principal, the special education teacher, and of course yourself. The pamphlet specifies a certain amount of days allowed for each step of the process and the laws governing it are very specific.

Should correcting the problem take more than the set period of time, mediation or arbitration might follow next.

If you have followed each step in the book, there is a chance that you will win your case. Winning the case might include the school having to pay for a private school of your choice and the transportation to get there. It might include teachers working with your child one on one or other pertinent activities. Unfortunately, many parents find out about their rights when the child is in middle school and much time is lost.

The Individuals with Disabilities Education Act (IDEA) said that all students should be educated "in the least restricted environment possible" (U.S. Department of Education, 2004). The child study team may insist that the child be in "the least restrictive environment" without mentioning "the most appropriate education." That might mean that if Johnny is not reading at grade level between third and fourth grade, he might be receiving "the least restrictive environment" without receiving "the most appropriate education." In this example, the most appropriate step might be to have Johnny placed in a resource room; it is a more restrictive environment but more appropriate. If Johnny spends an hour a day in the resource room to get extra reading and writing done and that doesn't work, then the next placement might be an all day special education classroom or a private school that specializes in Dyslexia and other issues.

Another thing that parents are often not aware of is that if your child has more moderate-to-severe special needs, then the school must, by law, continue to educate your child in a summer program called an ESY, or "EXTENDED SCHOOL YEAR." You are eligible to get an ESY only if your child has an IEP and if the school break would cause the child to fall behind in their school work. I cannot tell you how many parents are so thrilled to learn about that kind of a program when their child is moderate-to-severely autistic (or even children with speech delays, kids in wheelchairs, etc.) because when it comes to the summer, there is almost nowhere to go with these children. They do not fit in at camps, cannot play on the playground unattended, don't do well with the high temperatures in the summer sun, many do not sit in movie theaters, and some are OK with swimming (but many are not), and yet they can all benefit from a good intensive program. In the last five years, programs have begun to open up at a few of the YMCA centers and camps, but it is certainly not enough to address the needs of this population.

Section 504 Program

Among basic services that schools give to certain students on a regular basis are speech therapy, physical therapy, occupational therapy, and adaptive gym. Your child might be eligible for basic skills in a resource room and *might* also be eligible for a kind of social skills group therapy. Even non-special needs children who are not found to be eligible for these services under special education can receive great extra help under something called a 'Section 504 program'.

In an article by Mary Durheim entitled "*A Parent's Guide to Section 504 In Public Schools*," on the website GreatSchools.org, Section 504 is stated as being "a part of the *Rehabilitation Act of 1973* that prohibits discrimination based upon disability. Section 504 is an anti-discrimination, civil rights statute that requires the needs of students with disabilities to be met as adequately as the needs of the non-disabled are met." Also, an 'impairment' is defined and is described as follows: "An impairment as used in Section 504 may include any disability, long-term illness, or various disorder that 'substantially' reduces or lessens a student's ability to access learning in the educational setting because of a learning-, behavior- or health-related condition. ['It should be emphasized that a physical or mental impairment does not constitute a disability for purposes of Section 504 unless its severity is such that it results in a substantial limitation of one or more major life activities' (Appendix A to Part 104, #3)]" (Durheim, 2010).

The website article continues to state that, "Many students have conditions or disorders that are not readily apparent to others. They may include conditions such as specific learning disabilities, diabetes, epilepsy, and allergies. Hidden disabilities such as low vision, poor hearing, heart disease, or chronic illness may not be obvious, but if they substantially limit that child's ability to receive an appropriate education as defined by Section 504, they may be considered to have an 'impairment' under Section 504 standards. As a result, these students, regardless of their intelligence, will be unable to fully demonstrate their ability or attain educational benefits equal to that of non-disabled students (*The Civil Rights of Students with Hidden Disabilities* under Section 504 of the *Rehabilitation Act of 1973*—Pamphlet). The definition does not set forth a list of specific diseases, conditions, or disorders that constitute impairments because of the difficulty of ensuring the comprehensiveness of any such list. While the definition of a disabled person also includes specific limitations on what persons are classified as disabled under the regulations, it also specifies that only physical and mental impairments are included, thus 'environmental, cultural and economic disadvantage are not in themselves covered' (Appendix A to Part 104, #3)."

Author Mary Durheim goes on to say in her article *"Section 504 — just what exactly is it?"* "You've probably heard about it, but every school district addresses Section 504 in a different manner. Some districts have even been heard to say, 'We don't do that in this district.' But in fact, compliance to Section 504, which is a federal statute, is *not* optional. This article attempts to answer basic questions pertaining to the implementation of

Section 504 in public school systems" (2010). According to her article: A school is not required to evaluate a child under Section 504 just because a parent asks them to. Unlike special education, federal regulations under Section 504 do not require parents to be a part of the decision making. Each school district decides on the procedures for implementing Section 504. No formalized testing is required for Section 504. Schools can look at the child's report cards over the last several years, state assessment scores, and health records, in order to make their determination. The child who receives a Section 504 must have some impairment. That can be as simple as a learning disability, Dyslexia, all the way to a physical disability including speech impediment, low vision, hearing impairment, or being wheelchair-bound.

Under 504, accommodations such as untimed tests, highlighted text books, peer assistance with note-taking, extra textbooks for home use (please note: some schools have been eliminating textbooks altogether, so this may not apply), computers, enlarged print, behavior intervention plans, oral testing, visual aids, homework help, and many others … it is very open-ended[xiv].

Although there seems to be ample opportunity for the school to assist your son or daughter throughout their school day, I'd like you to focus on what is between the lines and unspoken regarding Section 504. If you notice in the beginning of the text on Section 504, it says every school district "addresses Section 504 in a different manner. Some districts have been heard to say, 'We don't do that in this district'," (Durheim, 2010). The point is that you are at the mercy of whether or not your school chooses to implement a 504. Though it is a federal statute, if your school district does not follow it, then you might have a difficult time making sure your child's civil rights are being met. I have seen many individual cases where a teacher makes promises to a family time and again, year after year, and in the end nothing is done to help the struggling child. If that same parent goes into school knowing the law about Section 504, then all of a sudden, phone calls are made and new people appear from the district ready to at least cooperate with you. No longer are the promises left to a subjective classroom teacher. However, and this is tricky, if the school does not agree with accommodating your child under 504, the parent may request a "due process hearing" or file a complaint with the

Office For Civil Rights. Since the Section 504 has been left up to the individual district's decision makers, is your only option to go to a "due process hearing?" A "due process hearing" is a very serious matter and very few parents ever have a chance of winning; but more about that later.

Frequently Used Terms

There are frequently used terms that would be to your benefit to become familiar with. The following terms sometimes can be used to intimidate you, the parent. If you, the parent, says to a child study team, "I think my child needs more help and I'm not happy with his/her progress," some of the staff may blurt out "Well, the law says we have to keep YOUR child in the 'least restrictive environment." That unwittingly backs the parent off; they somehow interpret that statement as "It's against the law the give that child more help," because it would go against "least restrictive environment." Another example may be when the staff says, "We have this handicapped class with five severely autistic kids who are pre-verbal down the hall, or, we have the inclusion class where she is now with an aide. We don't have anything else." In a way, they are "breaking the law" because they are not supposed to take a child and fit them conveniently into a program; rather, they are supposed to create or generate a program that fits the child.

These important terms are[xv]:

Adaptive Physical Education (APE) – a specially designed gym class that might help a student with developmental disabilities to learn to catch and throw a ball, balance that ball, and develop coordination.

Accommodations – anything that helps a child keep up or participate with other students such as extended time for tests; for example modifying the homework assignments by reducing the amount, allowing for a child to have a learning buddy they can talk to during class time.

Assessment or Evaluation – testing done to determine the placement of a struggling student struggling for a Section 504 or an IEP if they meet the special education criteria.

Behavior Intervention Plan (BIP) – a written plan that addresses the child's specific actions or behaviors; the plan will include positive steps to take if the child's behavior becomes disruptive.

Note: I had a student who was very

disruptive and had a special education plan, but was mainstreamed into the regular classroom. He had a tendency to pace around the room when the other children were seated and began to work. He had periodic meltdowns several times a week where he would cry or whine out loud for one reason or another as to why he was unwilling to do the work. Along with the parents and the child study team, a great plan was eventually implemented. He received a physical pass that gave him the right to just get up and walk out of the classroom, but only 3 times a week. That meant that instead of getting punished for his meltdowns – that seemed like he could not control – he was left in a position of having to self-monitor and self-evaluate. He would have to stop and think, "Is the frustration and anxiety that I'm experiencing so severe that I have to use one of my pass privileges, or can I wait?"

Child Study Team – a group that evaluates a child's level of performance in reading, writing, and arithmetic and can assess the child for the need for special education. If a child is found to be eligible for special education, the child study team will construct a formal individual educational plan. The team includes classroom teachers, educational specialists, parents, learning disabilities consultants, and school psychologists. The parents may bring an advocate of their choice.

Designated Instruction Services – extra instructions not typically found in a regular class may be part of a resource room or therapy.

Differential Standards for Graduation – a term that permits the school to graduate a child that cannot read or write because after all, the child is in "special education;" the standards are modified.

Disability – any physical, mental, or psychological impairment that limits or affects major life activities.

Due Process – a process where parents disagree with the recommendations of the school district; the parent must put their disagreement in writing within 30 days of filing any dispute. This may be resolved in a hearing or mediation.

Early Intervention – any program that assists developmentally delayed infants and toddlers to help prevent problems as the child matures; all public schools are required to have developmental disabilities programs starting the day the child turns three. Though in actuality the schools do not have it; it is because the parents are unaware that they are entitled to it.

Note: the author uses this term to describe any speech/OT/PT/art therapy in the early primary grades.

Extended School Year (ESY) – the school is required to continue the special education services during the summer if coming to an educational stop would be detrimental to the child.

Free Appropriate Public Education (FAPE) – special education services provided by the school without charge to the parents.

Inclusion – term used to describe special education students remaining in the regular classroom with supports such as an aid.

Individuals with Disabilities Education Act (IDEA) – see earlier in this chapter for full definition

Individual Education Plan (IEP) – a written document that states goals, objectives, accommodations, and materials used for students receiving special education.

Independent Educational Evaluation (IEE) – an assessment of the child's eligibility for services if a parent rejects or disagrees with the findings of the child study team; the parent has a right to bring non-school evaluators that the public school district could pay for. There is a controversy. Many schools pay for the IEE, but some districts find ways not to pay for it.

Individualized Family Service Plan (IFSP) – a plan that is written from infancy to the age of three to help your special needs child develop skills and can provide different therapies; most parents do not realize that if their child shows any signs or symptoms of a developmental or physical disability, the school must, by law, provide a program overall. Most schools provide preschool handicap classes including a bus that picks your child up at your house and drops them off. Even a child with a moderate lisp can qualify. More often than not, the preschool handicap classes are generally great programs.

Individualized Transition Plan (ITP) – (starts at the age of 14) helps guide an individual child toward skills required when high school is completed; it ranges from after school activities and daily living schools. For example, if a child has extreme deficits and is not going to make it to college, the ITP will give information leading towards the child acquiring job skills.

Least Restrictive Environment (LRE) – reviews placement options for special needs children such as the placement of a child in the mainstream/inclusion program with the support of an aid versus a resource room pull out several times a day with more intensive and modified instruction. The author would like to caution the family on this point; the real value of an LRE comes when it includes the "most appropriate education in the least restrictive environment." For example, Johnny is not able to learn to read without the help of an aid in a regular classroom, his IEP gets changed to say "Johnny will receive reading in a resource room two periods a day," and therefore the resource room is a more restrictive environment than the regular inclusive classroom. In this sense, restrictive is not negative; rather, it is beneficial if the child will get all of that help. Some schools tend to the throw terms around such as "least restrictive," but it takes it out of the context it was meant to be in.

Mainstreaming – this describes classrooms that have both regular children and special needs together; it used to imply that a child with special needs would be in the regular classroom for part of the day and in a special education classroom for the rest of the day, based on his or her own skills. Today, more often than not, it appears to mean when a special education student is in a regular classroom most, if not all of the day.

Manifestation Determination – a document that requires a school to determine if a child's behavior was caused by a disability or if the bad conduct in question was a result of the school district's failure to implement the IEP; a school cannot change a child's placement until this is investigated.

Multiple Disabilities – a combination of disabilities that causes special educational needs; it can be in the extreme of help for children who are both deaf and blind, all the way to children who have learning disabilities with emotional needs.

Non-public School (NPS) –if a child's disabilities are so severe or unique that the school cannot provide appropriate services, then the public school must pay for the private school with services; for example, schools that specialize in Dyslexia , Autism, and behavioral/emotional issues.

Obsessive-Compulsive Disorder (OCD) – an anxiety disorder that is pervasive and shows up to such an extreme, that it interferes with the thought processes and with a child's ability to learn. Children with this have ritualistic behaviors such as touching a door knob 100 times, tying and untying shoelaces, etc. The exciting and new information on OCD correlates children with this behavior having a history of strep throat, it appears that when OCD suddenly shows up, it is because of strep throat and is somewhere curable proved through use of certain antibiotics and adding properties to the blood. See also PANDAS (soon-to-be PANS) in this chapter.

Occupational Therapists – while some definitions say that occupational therapists provide consultation and support to staff to improve a student's fine/gross motor skills, the author believes that the occupational therapists are to work 1-on-1 or in small groups with the children (not as a consultant, but rather hands on) helping the child grip a pencil, follow dotted lines, catch and throw a ball, locate where they are in space, and so on.

Oppositional Defiant Disorder (ODD) – a child who defies authority to an extreme for more than 6 months and often occurs with other behavioral problems, ADHD, learning disabilities, and anxiety disorders.

Note: The author would like to point out that the numbers of children labeled "ODD" have gone up significantly. The author would like to point out that the climate of schools are changing, i.e., large proportions of the population are subdued and medicated and the children are taught more how to "follow rules" than experiment with learning. Within this context, any child who disagrees with authority gets quickly labeled.

Parent Consent – parent is informed and signs documents regarding the special education of their child.

Physical Therapist – helps a child gain gross motor skills such as jumping, running, riding a tricycle, etc. Some definitions claim physical therapists provided consultation and support to staff to improve a student's outcome, but a child in need of physical therapy need hands-on physical therapy and not just a mere consultation.

Residential and Private Placement – part B of the IDEA says that the local public school district does not have to pay for services at a private school if the district had free appropriate public education available to your child (they do have to pay if they did not have those services at the district).

Resource Specialist – those who provide modified instruction, working at a slower more comprehensive pace, to students who have an IEP.

Resource Specialist Program (Resource Room) – a room with materials, books, toys, computers, and brightly colored activities (full of resources) that enable a qualified special education teacher to assist your child in reading, writing, and math; it is an intensive program that should help children thrive.

School Psychologists – they have a variety of responsibilities from identifying and testing a child for intellectual, social, emotional, and behavioral needs, as well as providing programs to help the child. They might have lunchtime social skills groups for children who have difficulty connecting. They are usually required to be at a school IEP meeting.

Specific Learning Disability – special education term that identifies when a child has difficulty with language – spoken or written – that may interfere with the ability to listen, read, write, spell, speak, or perform mathematics.

Speech/Language Impairments – this is a communication disorders that interfere with language such as a lisp, stuttering, inability to articulate, or having problems with the voice.

Sensory Processing Disorder – can cause a child to misinterpret sensory information from sounds, movements, or touch. Some children with SPD may seek out intensive sensory experiences or get overwhelmed from normal amounts. For example, a slight smell in the room might cause a child to cry or hide in the closet; a regular child may go to shake the hand of the sensory-impaired child and the child may try to strike the first child automatically.

Speech and Language Therapists (Speech Therapists) – assess children for delayed speech and language skills; they help children enunciate beginning, middle and ending syllables, help with phonology, syntax, and general communication.

Special Day Class (SDC) – also known as a Multiple Disabilities Class, this is a self-contained special education class that provides services to students whose needs cannot be met by the general education program.

Tourette's Syndrome – when a child has multiple motor and/or vocal ticks that are uncontrollable and repetitive. Symptoms sometimes appear between the ages of 3- and 10-years of age.

Note: The author says that at times these symptoms appear within weeks of intensive vaccinations.

Transition IEP – IDEA mandates that by age 16, an IEP is to include goals and services for post secondary activities; this is merely the same as an ITP.

Workability Program – a program in writing for high school students to be able to successfully transition to employment, and/or quality adult life opportunities.

Disclaimer: This list is not to be construed as a specific legal list of terms, rather as a more practical hands-on type of guide. Please note that these terms were surprisingly difficult to explain and list because some are used within certain school districts and other terms are used in other school districts; there's no continuity.

Consider this chapter to be the instruction manual that your special needs child can come with. After all, this chapter – from the Section 504 to the IEP – is based on actions you **CAN** take within the school system.

Chapter 10: Education Issues

Inclusion

Years ago, special needs children were removed from the regular classrooms or the school. They were placed into a "resource room" with a small number of children. Sometimes these special needs children were sent to private schools or facilities paid for by the district. In resource rooms the children received a lot of individual attention and could work at their own pace.

Basically, schools used to have special education classes of kids who needed extra help all day, a qualified special education teacher, and usually an aid would be working all day with about five or six children. The kids would receive a large amount of therapy from experts hired by the school to come in to the classroom; they would offer speech therapy, physical therapy, and occupational therapy, and these would be part of the daily routine. Much of the time, the child would receive these services one-on-one several times a week. It would be a group effort between the teachers, the aides, and the therapists. Sometimes these children were even taught to learn to ride a bike or learn how to throw a ball. These intensive services cost the school more money than what was spent on a regular classroom. They had to have the teacher and an aid dedicated to such a small group and their own classroom, plus pay the therapist to be on site. In cases where a school did not have these services or a child had very severe problems, the schools would pay for the child to go to another special education public or private school and also pay for transportation. Then one day, the concept of "inclusion" came into play.

Approximately twenty-five years ago, a new theory of education came around called Inclusion. Inclusion was the concept that children should stay in the classroom with their regular peers. Schools loved this idea because it allowed them to slash their budgets. They were also able to avoid paying for resource rooms and private schools. They replaced the therapies with inclusion for nearly all children but it is particularly disappointing to see how they have done this with little children in first, second, and third grade.

"Inclusion" was a dream come true for the district; it claimed that all children could be taught in the regular mainstream classroom. Parents were told that their child would no longer be segregated from the rest of society and that they would learn just like all of the "regular" children

… that all the "regular" children would accept and respect them. Parents were promised that their child would learn with the "normal" kids.

Parents were thrilled to hear that their severely disabled child would be in a "regular" classroom; they frantically called each other and remarked about how well their children were doing and such, but nothing could be further from the truth. Parents loved this idea until they discovered their children were not making progress. What actually happened was that the child was placed in the back of the room with an aide. Although they received high grades on their report cards, they were not able to read and write, as the aide read to them.

Some parents think this is better than segregation into a resource room, but the actual purpose of the resource room was to catch them up to their peers. Mainstreaming is a concept in which a child may be in a regular math class but need a resource room for writing. I am all for inclusion when it means the child is able to keep up with their peers when learning and when they can read and write on their own. With intensive instruction in a resource room, they can learn to read and write.

Often, the inclusion program was void of speech, physical, and occupational therapies. Parents rarely found out how many services their children really lost out on until it was too late! They came to accept that, because of Autism or learning disability or Dyslexia, their child not being able to read was the "norm."

In actuality, it seems that these children are more *isolated and secluded* than included. Even though these kids are part of the classroom, they are not included when most of their classmates have play dates, birthday parties, or sleepovers; in some cases, these children became afraid to go to school functions and were often bullied.

Unfortunately as these children get older and their needs are not met, they can become aggressive and act out. In the news, more and more stories pop-up about how 5-year-olds are being handcuffed, arrested, and so on; what these children really need are small classrooms with therapy and "good behavior plans."

Some schools have hired people to come in with restraining devices. If only these schools had these resource rooms and the child had learned to read, they would not need these restraining devices. It would have been so much more cost effective, if they had taught them when they were younger in an appropriate class setting with a supportive staff, then they would not have had to resort to such devices. To my knowledge, 20 years ago most schools did not have to resort to restraining devices.

Scanning the news, it can be seen that monthly there are cases where such children wind up dying as a result of the school's inability to manage them. These people did not have their needs met when they were younger, such as small group support, behavior management programs, anti-bullying measures, school psychology help, etc. If so many programs were not terminated, these kids would have had the support and nurturing they needed when they were young. It doesn't matter if you are conservative or liberal; we all suffer in the long run from the consequences.

It is so sad to see schools tying children up with restraining devices or having the children sent away to institutions when the money could have been spent giving them the intensive services they needed when they were little. It is like being penny wise and pound foolish. I take a stand that with the correct and early implementation of services, most of these children would be reading and writing, and *growing* social skills. To approve of inclusion is the current fad and "politically correct" thing to do, but I assure you that there's a time to bring your child back into the mainstream – for subjects such as science and social studies – when, and only when your child is able to read and write.

Parents, do not give up on this and do not settle for your child not being able to read and write. In the rare cases where it is not an option, you can circumvent this problem with the use of today's technology such as laptops, iPads, and applications and typing programs that speak for the child. There are many children who have never spoken nor had the ability to read or write that sat looking empty to most people but suddenly came to life by the use of technological advances. You would be amazed at how these children that were never able to make verbal communication or defined interaction can suddenly came to journal their entire life's experience with the push of the button. A child that seemed so cut off from emotions remembers every single little detail despite the fact that for the majority of their lives they were crying and banging their heads. Most of them have very strong reception; like a radio, most of them have very strong reception but they cannot transmit.

Phonics

As explained in the previous chapters, approximately 25 years ago, children were taught the art of sounding out words. They broke words into syllables. They learned the rules of phonics. A new theory was developed at that time called "whole language." In whole language, children memorized words on flash cards. They were encouraged to spell the words any way they wanted. This was called "inventive spelling". This appeared to be a good thing at first, because children sounded like they had read a variety of books. They weren't really reading, rather they memorized the books. You can tell when your son or daughter has memorized a book by turning to a random page. You may notice that they cannot read it when it is isolated from the rest of the book. Whole language encouraged the child to "figure out the story by looking at the pictures." As the children get older, the books have fewer pictures and more words. Spelling tests are given in third grade and a child who is permitted to write the word "was" as "wz" was then told that they must unlearn it and learn it correctly. For an average child, this may be a moderately simple task but for a dyslexic child it is frustrating if not impossible.

Parents are frequently called around the end of second grade to be informed that a child study team would like to assess the student. This is not by accident. Learning disabilities and other headings work on the premise that the child's academic skills must be below grade level by approximately two years before they look at assessing or creating an IEP. Rather than help the children who are

struggling in first and second grade in resource rooms with a lot of attention, it seems as if they wait until the end of second grade to contact parents. Many schools receive up to $100,000 per child that gets classified in "special education." Some of these children would *not* have needed special education services had they been exposed to phonics in the very beginning.

Do you remember the TV commercial for "Hooked on Phonics?" What they did was recreate a phonics system that was previously used and turned into something new. Parents purchased the product at a cost of $250 or more only to find out they had to sit with the child at least an hour a day teaching the method. Few parents can sit with their child an hour a day for several reasons. With both parents often working full time there can be an issue with scheduling. Additionally, the child wants the parent to be a *parent* and the teacher to be a *teacher*. If a parent is lucky enough to have a child that will cooperate with them for an hour a day, they might not have needed "Hooked on Phonics" in the first place. Today there are all sorts of phonics games on the computer, some being better than others. It depends on the individual child and his or her needs as to which ones will work.

Charter and Alternative Schools

Today more and more schools are being created as charter schools. These schools originated as alternatives for poor, struggling inner city youth. Many of these schools become so popular that entry is a matter of a lottery. Scores and performance in these schools have been going up. Parents tend to participate with the school more. The idea of alternative charter schools has been doing so well that they are no longer an alternative only for city kids but you can now find them all over the country.

While they are not perfect, children in them seem to be thriving. This may be in part because most charter schools use a "multi-age" creative environment. That is where children of different ages can learn the same subjects. Usually in a charter school, there are tables, couches, rugs on the floor, or sections of the rooms that can mimic your living room. They have different academic centers: a math center, a reading and writing center, a science center, and a history center. As the children go through the centers, they pick up work appropriate to their skill level in each subject. A student may be really high level in reading, may be a third grade student reading at a seventh grade level, while only doing math at the third grade level thus they work at the seventh grade level in reading and the third grade level in math. When a child finishes their work, they might be asked to buddy up with another student to help them. It is a microcosm that reflects society more than a regular school.

Usually in a regular public school, you are separated by age, regardless of ability, and a teacher at the front telling everybody to open their textbook and answer questions 1-5. Often charter schools tend to have themes; one school might focus on the environment and recycling. Instead of only reading from books, the students may learn about plant and fish life; they go outside and gather samples to put under a microscope. In some schools they are required to have a portfolio of work they have done during the year. Often they out perform public school students and have an easier time assimilating into the real world when they get older. However, there will always be children who require more structure, more rules, and enjoy being told what to do. For them, regular instruction in a public school may be best.

While I am particularly interested in educational philosophies and different kinds of programs such as homeschooling, charter schools, special education school, and so on, I want to keep the doors open to a large variety. It is the regular mainstream educational public school program that has become so watered down and ineffective. These public school institutions have become more of a place for children to follow rules and regurgitate exactly what is told to them and less of a place to develop critical thinking. I am not saying that it is the public school's fault or pointing a finger, but trying to keep special education students in the regular class, being responsible for sex education in the class, teaching anti-bullying (very important!), removing of parties such as Christmas in order not to offend anybody in particular, reduction of art and music programs, gym programs, what did we expect? We have created a weak hodgepodge. Remember, in this generation of children there are fewer parents at home raising a child; more often than not, both parents are working full time (if not a single parent household as if often the case nowadays) and the child has come from day care or nursery school and there is a sort of over institutionalization.

After all, by October of second or third grade, the children are being conditioned to pass a standardized test as the most important barometer of their entire education. Children seem to know more about their friend's guns, medications, divorces, car engines, than they do about foreign languages, geography, and how to help each other (which was once known as civics classes). In my eyes, first grade could be on how to get along, how to socialize, how to help each other, and once that is learned, academics can come flying in at an accelerated rate. Many of these kids are coming in crying for love and attention. We CAN do this! We can bring back humanity, purpose and ethics into the public school system because if we do not, it will continue to be a disjointed, fractured system where fewer and fewer kids will make it into college.

Higher Education

Colleges today are in great flux. Everyone knows that the costs are soaring. Community colleges used to be considered a place where weak students could go after high school as a second chance. Now that many colleges and universities cost between $30,000 and $50,000 per year, families have opted to have their kids go to the more affordable community colleges for the first two years and transfer to better schools for the second two. Thus, with the influx of brighter and better prepared students at these community colleges, the quality of education has increased as well. (Whichever way you choose, kids are coming out of college owing over $100,000 and it's a big future problem.)

There are many colleges that claim to have good programs that offer help to special needs children who have ADHD, sensory impairments, and Dyslexia. They have special education departments along with glossy pamphlets displaying these departments. I caution you to take a closer look at these schools. Some have very good programs while others do not. There are colleges now like the Beaumont College in Lancaster, Florida and the Landmark College in Vermont that are beginning to cater to the special needs population and are advancing. These schools are targeting the special needs population and are exclusively open for special needs students.

I anticipate that more colleges for special needs students will be created because of the shift in populations. Some of them are great, but remember most of all that you want them to be a good fit for *your* student because what is good for one may not be for another[xvi]. An example would be when your child selects a school in the Northeastern part of the United States but dislikes the snow and cold. This might not seem important at first but it will become critical to whether they complete a degree.

Colleges have been raising their fees and scrambling for their attendants. In 1970s New York, city colleges were free. Scholarships were abundant for many kids, including students who did not get straight "A's." But today, an average college costs are extremely high, which accumulates around the hundreds of thousands in four years. It is becoming completely unimaginable. In the meantime, two year community colleges – once laughed at – and often considered a glorified repeat of high school, have risen to the occasion in part because their tuition could be as low as a few thousand a year.

It is not just about the money, there is a healthy experimental approach to opening new courses within community colleges that may be lacking at the larger, four-year institutions.

For example, classes in the Holocaust and Genocide studies, restaurant management, and how to grow your own food are now being offered. What are missing are classes in the practical side of the economy and money. There are plenty of classes in math and if you are interested in becoming a stockbroker, the skies the limit, but as far as preparing young people for the practical, everyday financial barometer, there is very little. With the US eroding its industrial base, regarding the course of events relating to the euro dollar, we are no longer preparing our young people properly to come out and turn things around from a leadership perspective. We must demand to see things turn around.

Some colleges are doing a great job of working exclusively with the special needs population and community. Landmark College is one shining example; it's been around since the 1980s and has a beautiful campus. The Landmark College website states, "Landmark College was founded in 1985 as the first college in the nation devoted to serving students with learning disabilities and in particular, Dyslexia . Since the 1990s, the college has served increasing numbers of students with Attention –Deficit/Hyperactivity Disorder (ADHD) and since the new millennium, students with Autism Spectrum Disorders (ASD). We continue to add through our resource space on learning differences such as ADHD and ASD"[xvii].

In some special schools or with some special materials for your special needs child, parents can deduct the expenses. Landmark College says, "Deductibility of tuition and fees as medical expenses; Landmark College tuition fees and other associate expenses may qualify as a medical tax deduction. Other expenses may include room and board, books and supplies, a computer and certain travel costs. IRS publications 502-medical and dental expenses and 907- Tax information for persons with disabilities states: "You can include in medical expenses, the costs (tuition, meals and lodging) of attending a school that furnishes special education to help a child to overcome learning disabilities. A doctor must recommend that a child attend the school. Overcoming the learning disabilities must be incidental to the special education provided" (2012). Chapter 12 will have an interview with the president of Landmark College.

Educating a child no longer is just reading, writing, and arithmetic. With the abundance of special needs children, on the autistic spectrum having ADHD, Dyslexia, and other issues, we need to challenge the old model and open up loving, nurturing, and exciting circuits for different types of people to thrive. The "one size fits all approach" does not fit any longer. The education of the special needs population does not need to become second rate; it should not be an afterthought. The future of millions of people and perhaps billions of dollars depends on it.

According to the National Institute of Mental Health (NIMH), 80 percent of Americans with Autism are under the age of 18 and that we need to prepare for a million people who may be in need of significant care (Insel, 2012). Many of them will soon age out of the school system. A large number of these kids will leave high school being completely dependent on others for everyday things. They will be unable to live on their own, hold a job, drive a car, go grocery shopping, or pay their own bills. If they are lucky enough they will live at home with their parents. When the day comes their parents will no longer be there, what will their choices be? For some it may be group homes, for others it may be institutionalization, but whatever it is it will certainly cost our society untold amounts of money and burden all taxpayers.

It is said that two percent of the boys in the United States fit this criteria.

With the medical / psychiatric fields arguing that Autism has always been around and it is simply a matter of better diagnosis, you will find that as this population ages, this cannot be further from the truth. In England, some people have taken to establishing campuses and places of employment for this very ill population. They have opened restaurants completely staffed with autistic people. They cook and serve customers. This seems like a wonderful solution. There also are villages ready to assist the severely autistic population for the rest of their lives. To my knowledge, the United States does not accommodate this population. As usual, by trying to save money now, they will be spending much more in the future, in the next few years it will be an urgent matter.

Chapter 11: The Right to Health

Finding Efficient and Effective Expert Help Issues

A major problem concerning treatment of children is that if you take your child from expert to expert, the expert seems to be so focused on *their* own little niche as opposed to how the parts come together. A much more holistic systemic approach is necessary. An analogy to this situation would be the steps involved in building a house. The specialist who excavates is great at digging holes for the foundation, but knows nothing about the roof. The sheetrock specialist is great at putting up sheetrock, but knows little about how to provide electricity. It is the architect who knows all of the elements and how they need to fit cohesively together. What's missing when it comes to special needs is the *architect* – the person who knows all of the little parts and aspects, and can put them all together.

So just like thinking about the sheetrock expert who does not know electricity, we come to the example of the food allergist who knows allergies, but does not know of any other aspects of Autism or ADHD. You can find a great physical therapist that can improve your child's Hypotonia (reduced muscle strength and tone), and make the left and the right parts of the child's body equally strong, but she may not understand how the eyes track. She also may be unaware of how the food allergies disrupt the child's behavior and cause muscle weakness. These experts only understand their own small elements and do not know how they affect the whole child. There is a great need for better communication among the experts, but the system is fractured and disjointed. The child does not consist of individual parts. The child is a whole child, physically, emotionally, and mentally, and must be treated as such.

As another example, if you are lucky enough to find a good allergist who understands the chemical reactions with food, they most likely know little about the benefits of sounding out words using phonics versus whole language in a classroom. Their training is limited to the allergies and not the educational aspect affecting the child. Likewise, a good internist might not have much information about a good child study team. If you find a Special-Ed teacher who understands the benefits of phonics, their training will not encompass food allergies; they might not

be aware of skin impediments and gut issues from food allergies, which would affect attentiveness and behavior in class. Obviously, if special needs teachers had some guidelines for what to physically observe in a child, they would be able to understand that for example if a child has a skin rash, it more than likely will also affect the child's behavior and attentiveness. Digestive tract issues and allergies would be understood as being part of the systemic issues affecting the child's behavior in the long run. Many times teachers might notice that some children can be disruptive during certain times of the day, not realizing that these children ate something during lunch that was affecting their behavior because it setting off allergic reactions.

Thus you, the poor parent, are left hopping from specialist to specialist.

Unfortunately, many parents and experts alike do not know enough about all the many issues and connecting factors affecting special needs children and that in the long run to road to recovery of a child stems from a correct combination of all of the issues that are relevant to that particular child's issues and conditions. There is an art to knowing what and how much a particular child truly needs. It takes a complete holistic approach, from the top of the child's head literally to the tip of the child's toes to recover Autistic, ADHD, and learning-disabled children. This kind of professional is rarely found in allopathic mainstream medicine; and if you find an "architect of medicine" that can oversee other practitioners, I would be surprised to see if they accept medical insurance.

"Defeat Autism Now" (DAN) was formerly a group of practitioners that came together somewhere in the 1990s who believed that Autism could be cured with biomedical treatments. Today, these doctors are being known as biomedical treatment doctors biomedical. With their biomedical orientation, they understood that chemical toxicity and overload greatly affects today's children. There were yearly conferences that the public could attend with medical doctors that chose to be a part of the process of making children well again.

In general, I am in favor of families seeking out the help of a biomedical doctor, if their child has Autism. On the other hand however, caveat emptor – let the buyer beware! Although there are many wonderful practitioners, I have personally seen and known of a few doctors who charged large amounts of money, did not accept insurance, and within the matter of two or so years did not improve the health of the child. In fact, some of these doctors have published well-written alternative health papers, and are high within the organization. Just because this is the case – with well-written papers and high-ranking statuses – doesn't mean your child's condition will improve. So please, do your own homework. The best thing to do is locate a few families whose children did permanently improve. It is advised to go further than just simply taking the names off of the recent referral list. Again the author wishes to emphasize that what is best for the child is an individual approach.

When looking for a biomedical doctor, type in "how to find a biomedical doctor," or type in "where to look for a biomedical doctor conference"[xviii]; such conferences are where nutritionists, doctors, and physicians come together to find treatments in the biomedical and non-biomedical realm. It is difficult to find one great source, but as a starting point you can head to AutismOne.org; they are affiliated with the Autism File magazine and Autism One radio. It is a combined effort with the UK and the United States. It is interesting to note that while looking for legitimate sources to help the reader connect with a biomedical doctor, Shelley and her writing assistant came across the website ChildHealthSafety.wordpress.com show that "1 in 38 British boys have an autistic condition" as recently as 2009. It would be valuable for families with a newly diagnosed child to attend one of these conferences; in a recent one, there were over 1500 people in attendance, and raised the issue of mitochondrial disorders. Most of the people at the conference would have your best interest at heart.

Defining Special Needs

There is a growing concern regarding the subject of special needs and sick children. Up until now, there have been different terms and categories under the heading of "Autism." Much time and money has been spent on the various diagnostic criteria; at the high end, there is Asperger's Syndrome and/or High Functioning Autism (HFA). In this category, the people are generally very bright, but tend to be quirky. They have problems with their social skills and making and keeping friends. They not only look and sound geeky, but they often end up getting paid to "be" geeky. An example would be working for a big box electronic store helping to repair computers or being sent on an assignment to people's homes to set up their new home theater.

These people are also often object oriented and detail oriented. When younger, some of them could play with Lego's for up to eight hours a day. They have extraordinary memory in the things they are interested in and may speak incessantly about their areas of interest, regardless whether the other person is listening or not. This is one of their problems in socializing with other people.

Then there is Classic Autism that can include children at the very low end. This includes children who cannot speak, make eye contact, eat normally, read or write, children who may self injure or head bang can be in this group. There is also Pervasive Developmental Disability Not Otherwise Specified, PDDNOS, which represents a group of children who seem to have many symptoms of classic Autism but whose symptoms do not quite fit in well. An example may be a child who may head bang or vomit, perpetually fall, but have the capability of taking an object such as a spoon and pretending that it is an airplane. The classic autistic kids cannot do that and instead simply pretend to.

A larger group of children are labeled as having PDDNOS rather than being labeled as having Autism. The doctor might not want to bring bad news to the family and may diagnose PDDNOS as a way to circumvent the use of the word *Autism*. Or, the local school district does not have an Autism program, and therefore sends many of the children to doctors they trust will not diagnose the child with Autism. On the other hand, if a child is diagnosed with Autism (not PDD), then some schools are culpable and financially responsible to pay for Autism services. If the child is diagnosed as PDD, then many of the schools are not responsible to pay for services. Some special needs children are now losing services. What we have here is a social reason, an economic reason, a political reason, and a medical reason to get a particular diagnosis. Giving services to autistic or autistic-like symptoms is federally mandated. As more and more of these differentiating labels are dropped, new ones are taking their place such as Social Communication Disorder (SCD). SCD is an impairment of pragmatics, and is diagnosed based on difficulty in the social uses of verbal and non-verbal communication (American Psychiatric Association, 2012). The problem is that children who would have received services under Autistic Spectrum Disorder, ASD, will be diagnosed as having SCD, which has far less mandates for services. The danger here is that many of these kids might get speech and language therapies, but lose behavioral, physical, and occupational therapies. When they have a meltdown, there will be little to no emotional support.

As confusing as the system seems, it is in my opinion about to get dramatically worse. The Diagnostic and Statistical Manual of Mental Disorders (which is known as the DSM, published by the American Psychiatric Association) is about to remove all the different diagnoses and lump everything together as just plain "Autism.". While the newer publications are attempting to streamline and eliminate diagnostic terms, it appears that the psychiatrists have brought clarity

to the diagnoses, clarity that they will be reimbursed by insurance companies, but lacking clarity of the affects of numerous changes and services for the children.

Many articles have begun to appear on the advantages and benefits of people having Autism and how Autism has always been around. In fact, the term "ADHD" is now suddenly being written up as being part of the Autistic Spectrum. It is not. What seems to be happening is that we are being manipulated to believe and accept that between 16 and 20% of autistic children are somehow "normal." Articles on the qualities of the high end are abounding. Yet the DSM is also planning on adding hundreds of new diagnostic criteria to children. Then too, a flood of new medications arises with possible negative effects as the patent on a particular drug comes to an end. It's kind of like circular thinking; as the patent (monopoly) of a particular drug comes to an end, a host of new formulations and medications are marketed to replace the high moneymaking the company was to have because of the patent. Some would say why not just create new medical diagnoses that supports the new drug?

There was a film released more than 25 years ago called "Famous people with Dyslexia ," but I noticed recently that the name was changed to "Famous People with Autism." Watching all those parents write in to thank the filmmakers for showing the qualities of famous people with Autism, it was disheartening because little do they know that it was Dyslexia and not Autism. Recently, I tried to look up this phenomenon and I discovered some researchers making a name for them for having "published" a new research

paper that re-identified the symptoms of Dyslexia and ADHD as being the same symptoms of Autism.

In fact, in the past five years or so, I have seen so many little boys diagnosed as Autistic, OCD, PDD, and ADHD, and medicated for each one of those terms. I could see this coming, that the term ADHD and Autism would become interchangeable. It is to no one's advantage. My purpose for having these children accurately diagnosed is to give them as many therapies and skills when they're young in order to drop the diagnosis when older because of the child's behavior, academics, and social skills. My purpose is not just to keep a label but also to quicken the pace and getting the child so well as to be able un-label them.

In my article, *"Childhood has Become a Diagnosis Game,"* I state, "It used to be that childhood kids played games like hide n' seek and 'tag, you're it"[xix]. The games sadly have changed. Today the game is what plethora of illnesses are the children are being diagnosed with?. Autism and ASD or Autism Spectrum Disorders; ADD or Attention Deficit Disorder; ADHD or Attention Deficit Hyperactivity Disorder, ODD or Oppositional Defiance Disorder; OCD or Obsessive Compulsive Disorder; Sensory Integration issues; and the list goes on and on. We have gotten to the point that letters in the alphabet stand for illnesses more than reading and writing.

So let's take a closer look and attempt to examine what might be happening. One of the issues at play is that the diagnosis of children is not quite as standardized as you might think. Take a child who cries, talks back, cannot seem to eat properly or make friends and seems to run around the classroom a lot. In town A, he or she might be diagnosed as having ADHD. Now take the same child to town B with the same symptoms and on the same day the child might be labeled as having a form of Autism, particularly because the socialization is weak. Take the same child to yet another town and the child will receive yet another diagnosis. There really is no blood test or scan for these illnesses. A behavioral profile is filled out and a clinical judgment is made.

I have seen children who are age six give up to five different diagnoses, such as ADD with hyperactivity, ODD, OCD, and bi-polar disorder. At this point, medications are prescribed several at a

237

time; one for the day, others for the night. Some local public schools offer classes for the growing Autistic populations – all day handicapped programs. In those neighborhoods guess what might be diagnosed? High Functioning Autism (HFA), or Asperger's another form of Autism. In neighborhoods that offer Inclusion only, with an aide, a more general term might be given such as Learning Disability (LD).

There are other areas of concern. When a child receives multiple diagnoses, or Co-Morbid labels, such as ADHD, OCD, Bi-Polar at the same time, it is often in an effort to avoid the term of Autism. By avoiding an ASD, the school does not have to open a program exclusively for Autistic children. How did we get to the point where so many children receive a diagnosis? With the push for medications along with the exposure of toxic chemicals being routinely injected into our children, we have been seeing an increase in diagnoses. Twenty or so years ago Autism was rare. Today, you can go see these children at school, in the parks, at the libraries and even while food shopping.

The latest findings show that it may be as high as one in every 38 children. I estimate it is even a greater number, having worked with special needs children for 25 years. If you can claim that children have multiple illnesses often enough, what can the result be? For one thing, we may see in about five years from now, articles stating that the numbers of Autistic children have gone down. The numbers are not really on the decline; rather the 'Diagnoses Game' has increased.

Having been a member of the International Dyslexia Association for nearly two decades, I wondered how this could happen. Upon looking into it from some very basic and accessible sources, I saw that Wikipedia listed a definition for Autism, Jan. 17, 2009 as, "a brain disorder characterized by impaired social interaction and communication." In the *Autistic Spectrum Disorders Fact Sheet*: "Researchers claim that (Dyslexia) is a brain-based condition… they might be labeled as having a 'behavior problem'" (Fact Sheet: *Dyslexia a co-morbid disorder associated with Autism Spectrum Disorders*).

I will be the first to admit that there is an overlapping of symptoms. Thus, a child that has trouble making eye contact and forming relationships might have an ASD or might just have a social problem that is common with Dyslexia. Dyslexia is not simply reversing letters or numbers. It is a, "Processing of information problem in the Auditory, Visual or Kinesthetic Mode" (Tzorfas, What is Dyslexia , 2008). Many dyslexics have difficulty with reading other people's emotions or subtle cues. This year I have not seen one child in my non-medical opinion properly diagnosed. The boundaries have eroded.

One child thought to be on the ASD Spectrum was Dyslexic and had anxiety. Another diagnosed ADD had Dyslexia. One child had no diagnoses but kept a poker face, did not interact, and behaved as if he was the only person in the room. Being disconnected and lacking empathy or a basic connection with everyone puts him at risk for a diagnosis of Asperger's Syndrome. Even when asked to express his feelings, he had no ideas. He did not know what one feeling to the next was.

As previously discussed in the book, sometimes hyperactive children might actually have a systematic Candida infection because they have taken antibiotics. The antibiotic's job was to kill the bad bacteria, the infection, but they simultaneously killed off the good bacteria. This is when the bad bacteria start to grow and take over. Yeast develops. Yeast creates a situation in which children crave sugar, wheat, and foods such as pasta and pizza. Those foods enable the yeast to grow and multiply in the billons. The carbohydrates convert to sugar once ingested. Many nutritionists agree that those foods should be eliminated. Some feel that by eliminating them, the yeast infection will be cured. I disagree. An active yeast infection takes

far more than a simple change in diet.

Health food stores and experts such as Gary Null and those that practice homeopathy, also known as Naturopathic Doctors (ND), may recommend Caprylic Acid supplements, garlic which is an anti-fungal, grape seed extract, and others.

Additionally, if you have a young teen and try to change their diet, removing sweets and pizza might be impossible. Sure, you can get them to cut back, but to stop it entirely is way easier said than done. In *Help for the Hyperactive Child* by Dr. William G. Crook, you can see at a glance with triggers yeast as well as what behaviors may be involved. The book is laid out clearly and is easy to digest. The yeast-infected child might easily be misdiagnosed and medicated. Psychologists and psychiatrists are often not trained in these issues. It is up to the parents to look into what is best for their children.

Parents could learn to trust their instincts. The conservative thing to do is to try to find out if yeast is playing a part in the disruptive behavior. If, for example, a child has had several ear infections and then had tubes placed in the ear, it is likely that the child has several rounds of antibiotics leading to an internal yeast issue. The yeast could be cured from the inside out.

In today's society one does not look far for children with problems. The younger the child is when issues are addressed, usually the better the outcome. Part of the problem is because of the diagnoses game. It seems as time goes by just about anyone can play. Teachers recommending, doctors mentioning what medication to consider, plus neighbors, friends and families pointing out issues is great.

Finally with all the pharmacological television commercials, kids are now diagnosing each other. 'Mom, do I have restless leg syndrome?' 'Mom, do I have a social anxiety disorder? I think I need my doctor right away.' Illnesses have nearly become the norm and that is something that can make anyone feel true discomfort"

The topic of health concerns way more than what medication or what diagnosis do your children have. Mental Health Diagnosis is only valuable for a young child when the goal is to give them all sorts of therapeutic services in effort to recover them from the need for a diagnosis. Health is more than a pill. There's room for a pill if that pill makes the child 85-90% better; unfortunately, with co-morbid diagnoses, there has been a "co-morbid sense of multiple prescriptions."

The Canary Party

A number of health concerned people have recently united by becoming a member of the "Canary Party", which first began in the summer of 2011. The Canary Party was founded by a group of people from different parts of the country who came together and spoke on a common topic of how families are "sick and tired of being made sick and tired." They recognized that the large numbers of children who have ADHD, Autism, emotional disturbances, and learning disabilities symbolize that something is not right with our young population.

People who join the Canary Party are deeply concerned with the toxicity found in vaccines, food, water, air, and soil. They are deeply concerned with the overuse of prescription drugs, the removal of vitamin supplements, the addition of genetically modified foods, the contamination with BPA, and the use of fluoridated water. They are alarmed at the increase in all types of cancer while not appreciating the barbaric usage of radiation and chemotherapy for cancer care. They addressed areas of health, safety, medicine, cancer, vaccines, and radiation in our environment.

The word "Canary" was chosen because of its significance to the dangers of everyday surroundings. Canaries are little yellow birds that were once sent down the shafts of coalmines to test the air quality to see if it was safe for people. If the canary did not return, then the air was poisonous and void of oxygen. If the canary did return, then it was likely safe to send the miners down for the day's labor. This generation of sick children is the equivalent of a "Canary in a Coalmine" that does not return. We see these illnesses everywhere, in every state and from every background since the late 1980s. Canaries have told us about environmental dangers in other ways. Take for example aluminum Teflon-coated frying pans. If you cook food at a high heat in a pan like this and happen to have a canary nearby in the kitchen, the canary would die from the gasses put off by the aluminum and Teflon when it reached a high heat.

The Canary Party goes way beyond politics and touches upon the health of human beings in this day and age. I had a chance to interview Ginger Taylor, the Executive Director of the Canary Party. When I asked Ms. Taylor how the Canary

Party came to be, she responded with "Mark Baxill, one of the top editors at *Age of Autism*, and editor at large, originally wrote about it over a year ago in 2010 and mentioned the term 'canary.' That is how the name came to be." She said that the canary is still used as a warning to people to this day.

I was curious as to how people around the country could get involved with the Canary Party[xx]. Ginger wanted more people to go as a spokesperson to Washington, DC to lobby for children's issues & safety, medical care, and vaccinations. "But it's the exhausted parents of vaccine-injured children that are too broke to go," she said. "The pharmacy industry hires shiny, well-fed and groomed representatives to go to Washington to lobby on behalf of the pharmaceutical and vaccine companies. WE need to find a middle ground to represent our concerns." This is a pressing issue and more people must get involved. Things will not change unless *people* do.

When speaking with Ginger about the health and care of autistic children, it was understood that more than 50% of children either do not get better or do not have their needs met. Ginger said, "If this was a large car mechanic company known for quickly lubricating and changing oil in a car, and the cars came out damaged and bad all around, the company would be taken to court immediately." When I re-read some of the notes from the interview, I found this to be particularly poignant and amusing because in this scenario, the cars would then have "leaky gut syndrome", as autistic children often do.

The Canary Party covers a wide range of concerns including but not limited to harmful vaccines, poor quality cancer care, radiation concerns, health insurance concerns from diabetes through heart disease, unsafe pharmaceutical products, the drugging of our children, senior care, and a plethora of other health and safety concerns. Other than perhaps pharmaceutical employees and medical doctors, who wouldn't be interested in this? Who doesn't have a relative with sub-optimal healthcare? *Everyone* has a problem.

Chapter 12: How to take a Vacation with a Special Needs Child

It is often difficult to get Autistic children and teens to adjust and transition to the simplest of things such as getting them from the car to the house and vice versa. Hopefully after following many of the practical steps in this book such as detox, adding early interventions, and "rebooting their brains", and so on, your family has reached a point where they are able once again to go on vacations.

Going on vacation with an Autistic child can be particularly difficult. You want to know what you are getting into. The hotel room must not have too many smells. If your child is the type that opens doors and runs, you want to be able to have control over the security of the doors and windows. The room cannot also be too noisy, such as being next to a construction site. Autistic and ADHD children often do better where there is an indoor swimming pool and an indoor playroom. Even if the indoor playrooms are particularly noisy, that is okay; most of these children can tolerate the noise of an electronic game. WIFI, Phone Apps, and Internet have become very valuable in this day and age.

When taking these children on vacation, it is preferable to have nearby restaurants on the premises or nearby restaurants that serve bland food in the surrounding areas. On the "must have" menu, there will be items such as chicken nuggets, French fries, hamburgers, and chicken soup. These children rarely do well when the smell of items like seafood and other delicacies are present. With this in mind, a few hotel chains have begun to consider accommodating special needs and their family. Also, some hotels are known for assisting the families. In some hotels, the staff even goes with the child to activities both on premises and off.

The Disney Corporation has begun to take the lead in accommodating special needs. They have programs where you make contact with them before your arrival. Disney also offers "Guests with Disabilities" passes that allow special needs visitors to avoid long lines. The Autism Society of America recently brought 2000 people to Disney.

The Disney Cruise Line has begun to accommodate special needs children in various ways. Some parents have taken their special needs children on a cruise with Disney's Oceaneer Club. According to the Disney Cruise website, "Disney's Oceaneer Club on the Disney Magic is a children's activity center located on Deck 5, Midship. Open from approximately 9:00 a.m. to midnight daily, Disney's Oceaneer Club is the ideal place for children 3 to 10 years of age to dress up as their favorite princess or hero, play games, use the computer lab and enjoy a wide variety of supervised activities throughout the day" (Disney, 2012).

Disney goes on to say that, "Inspired by Disney's *Peter Pan*, Disney's Oceaneer Club is designed to look like Captain Hook's pirate ship straight out of Never Land. Featuring a treasure chest-themed television set, lamps that resemble barrels, hanging ropes, wooden planks, and a glistening fiber-optic night sky, Disney's Oceaneer Club provides a wondrous setting for children to learn, play and interact with others while Mom and Dad are off on their own adventure" .

Other theme parks that have similar programs include Sea World and Busch Gardens. The Discovery Cove in Orlando offers swimming with dolphins to kids with special needs. Parents and family members should call at least four months ahead to make reservations, the park only accepts a limited number of visitors a day.

Other vacation hotspots to consider are places like Hershey Park in Hershey, Pennsylvania. Although many of the rides are off limits, children with special needs can get half-price admission during the summer season and bypass lines for all rides. Hershey prides itself in posting information about the ingredients in all of its foods on their website. They report where the foods are gluten free, egg free, peanut free, vegan and vegetarian.

Adaptive Sports Center of Crested Butte, Colorado offers activities to children with cognitive and physical disabilities. Skiing and snowboarding are some of the activities offered[xxi]. Always a great idea, if a child loves sea animals and water, are the variety of swimming with the dolphins programs throughout southern Florida.

The DRC (Dolphin Research Center) can accommodate children with various physical or mental challenges and life-threatening illnesses. They have programs such as dolphin encounter and dolphin dip, offering recreational interaction with both dolphins and sea lions. Private workshops and specialized equipment is available so that the "special needs program can help to remove the barriers that these children face." They are known for having a variety of activities; one is a five day program with recreational and motivational programs for children and adults with special needs. The DRC is a not for profit research and educational facility located on Grassy Key, Florida[xxii].

I interviewed Denis Richards of the website Water Planet (www. waterplanetusa. com), whose group was big enough to require a website in 2004. I was curious beyond what was printed and, since the animals are completely free in the wild and not penned-in, how Water Planet got its start. "Around 1996, a mother from Japan heard swimming with the dolphins could help autistic and handicap children. She brought her little girl to us. The mother said that after their return from swimming with the dolphins, the child's behavior did in fact improve, especially in school".

Then Denis added expressive art programs and music programs, and the whole program grew from that point on.

Denis wants people to understand that there is no magic to the dolphin or a known sonar therapeutic effect; he feels that telling parents that there is some "magical sonar effect" would be misleading. "Make it clear that there is no evidence that the dolphin would actually heal the child in any way," Denis confirmed. When I mentioned that there would be a therapeutic benefit just because of the relationship of the child to the dolphin, Denis agreed.

Water Planet provides two different kinds of programs; for the more physically challenged, they have the serenity program (close to $3,000), the price includes one child and one parent and incorporates more intensive therapies. It has Watsu Therapy which is akin to Aquatic Therapy (movement in water) and there are also music programs and behavioral programs, and it is very intensive. The parents often stay at Gulf Gate condominiums (not included in the initial price). There is a lot of safety equipment with these programs. The other program is called the harmony program. This also includes expressive art therapy and may include watsu and/or cranial sacral therapy, physical therapy and so on.

After asking Denis how he handles a child's meltdown and acclimates a child to swim in the water, he said generally what they do is give the child a chance by spacing out how the program evolves. He also said that he tries to have the families arrive in Florida on a Saturday, and meet with his staff on a Sunday. Generally, the kids can go to the pool Sunday while the parent meets privately because they might not want to speak in front of other families, as it is a private session. On

Monday, they begin to take the children into the water. The pontoon (a wider, more stable boat with two holes) will be beached if that group of children is too afraid to get into the water right away.

In that case, the children go "directly from the hard surface of the boat directly to the sand, for the children who are afraid of the water." Denis is very aware of how these children have trouble transitioning. Each child is assigned a trainer based on an affinity with that person; they watch to see how they connect with each other and the process is not predetermined. In my opinion, that process is absolutely fabulous.

Denis makes it clear when families apply that children who have no control and are a danger to themselves and others, do not participate in his program. "Parents are at our programs to control the children," Denis stated. Kids come in to the program as individuals or in groups. Sometimes there is a group for older kids – from the ages of 16-22 – but most of the kids are usually between the ages of 5 and 12. Denis said the maximum capacity on any boat is 18; that includes the staff and parents.

Other marine animals that the kids touch, see, and learn about might include starfish and crabs. Denis said, "We have a wet lab where the staff and parents dive down (waist deep), and catch these animals to show them to the children."

When Denis was asked how he gets kids who may have never been in the ocean before, to actually go into it, he said "By beaching them and playing with them, then splashing the water gradually the kids lose their fear of what may be under the water" (Richard, 2012).

Denis appears to have grown into this passion and acquired an insightful sense on how to be with an autistic child. I think that this might be a case where his respect and sensitivity of the sea life has trained him to be respectful and sensitive to human life.

Often times, the parents with special needs kids start and create these programs and bring them forward into a reality. The psychologists are not doing this, and we need more than that little room and so on.

Another exciting program is called "Autism on the Seas." This program is offered by Royal Caribbean International since 2007, who state, "We're dedicated to providing vacation and travel options for individuals and families living with Special Needs, including, but not limited to, Autism, Asperger's Syndrome, Down

Syndrome, Cerebral Palsy, and all Cognitive, Intellectual, and Developmental Disabilities" (Special Needs on Vacation, 2012).

I interviewed Jamie Grover. He is a Director of Group Development and a partner in the Autism on the Seas Company. He has a Master's degree in Social Work, and trained in the art of behavior modification, and is also a father of a young adult with Autism. His partner owned Alumni Cruises and was a huge fan of the sports team the Miami Dolphins; they invited Dan Marino who was a football player, and he came on the ship and spoke with some families. Let it be known that the Marino Foundation, established in the early 1990s, was founded after he and his wife received a diagnosis for their son, Michael. Jamie acknowledged that most kids cannot go on

vacation because of their behaviors that go along with Autism and other disabilities.

The first year, they designed a program for cruises for families with autistic children; they anticipated two cruises for the year. They actually ended up doing eight in total! Jamie said that they do not offer any therapies on the ship. He said, "after all, this is a vacation!" "If the child wants to do an activity that is fine. But if the child is going in circles as long as they are not hurting themselves or someone else, then we let them be," Jamie continued.

"The environment on a cruise ship is so different from the environment in school. I have seen moms crying as they watch a child perform a task that they could never do before. In school, they at times force children to do a certain activity; here, we don't," Jamie exclaimed.

251

"Sometimes in school or in certain certified therapies, the child is asked to do a particular activity for 20 minutes for this, 10 minutes for that, and 18 minutes for that, and the real world is not that way," Jamie continues. "The real world is continually changing. Some of these programs turn out 'robot-sounding children.' Our kids are like snowflakes, none of them are the same."

"Sometimes we have to go into their world, rather than forcing them to come into ours." Jamie's attitude is to have the families listen to everything that is out there – every doctor, every therapist – and then to take the pieces that relate to their child. The only time he feels that they shouldn't try everything out there is in the case where the cost is just too high and there is no proven outcome. Jamie cited oxygen therapy. Jamie wants parents to trust their gut instincts. He said that a psychologist who sits in the classroom observing your child and then writes a 15-page report has no more knowledge about your child than you do; you the parent, are the expert.

Jamie pointed out that on the cruise, there are some informal rap sessions where parents can speak with other people that have a lot of experience with a variety of subjects concerning Autism. They might ask questions from a person's expertise on the IEP or another person might be an expert in training dogs for children with Autism. "We do not pay the staff," Jamie says, "We provide the vacation in exchange for their assistance on the cruises. The majority of our staff is students working on a degree in child development. It could be in special education, psychology, pediatrician, and sometimes they are interns that need a certain amount of credit hours of experience."

When I asked Jamie if they would hire an ASD person to work on his ships, he said that they do not discriminate against developmental disabilities but that like everyone else, it is not a paid staff position. At one time, a family came on board whose son had HFA (high functioning Autism) and he recommended that the young adult should come on the ship on the next cruise. The mother was very concerned that her son could not travel without the family, but in fact he shared a room with his own son. Jamie said they had a great time and the boy being a part of the cruise was a great experience for all.

Jamie is excited to associate with a program that helps parents afford the cruise. Skyward Bound Ranch Charity based in Texas, helps provide financial assistance for families that would never be able to think of taking a cruise. They have a great "pay it forward" program. They also help the homeless and some schools.

Not only does Autism on the Seas hold cruises with Royal Caribbean, but also Carnival Cruises. The Skyward Bound Ranch Charity organization has also hosted iPad cruises; the ranch gives 25 iPads to families and an instructor will be on the cruises to teach the parents and the children how to use it. The iPads will have many apss, even an app on emotions (such as happy, angry, sleepy, etc.). Some of the cruises will be leaving from ports in New Jersey. iTalk.org is also affiliated with Jamie's programs.

Jamie said that he has met a bunch of families that come on the cruise and become close friends; they bond with other families they met that stay in contact for many years. The cruises attempt to integrate the kids with Autism with many of the activities but they also have some activities that are specifically set aside for the autistic kids. An example would be if the ship has ice skating; they give the autistic children private times because they may be new to it, while other families have often had prior experience and skate better than other children; autistic children often have physical anomalies as well such as clumsiness, weakness in some parts of their body and strengths in others, or hypotonia (when part of the body as low muscle tone). They like to have the kids tour the captains rooms, and it is always fun for them to get the private tour. "When the parents come on board, they often have concerns, especially the newly-

diagnosed," Jamie says. "Sometimes the parents speak of their child's echolalia and they ask 'How do I get my child's condition to stop?' and I respond 'Do not squash the echolalia because someday it might turn into real verbal communication'" (Grover, 2012).

Echolalia is when the child repeats word for word what is said to them much like a parrot repeating its owner's words. This condition does not imply that the child understands what is being said. If the parent says, "How are you?" the child repeats, "How are you? How are you? How are you?" Jamie feels that having the child repeat words is further advanced from a child that says absolutely nothing. He feels that their repeating words can possibly turn into normal speech one day in years to come and I full agree with that mentality; I believe we should also add to echolalia. Jamie likes to help build family dynamics and believes there should be support for siblings.

When I originally spoke with Jamie, I thought I was conducting just an interview about a ship and a cruise. What I really found was a man full of compassion and wisdom on the nature of individuals with Autism and the interaction with their families as well as others. He seemed to possess leadership qualities that I hope he can bring from port to port.

Years ago, parents with severely autistic children stopped trying to go on vacation; it wasn't worth the effort because the child perpetually melted down. Today, there are more and more places that are willing, able, and "wanting" to help children with special needs enjoy a vacation. With a little effort and research on the parent's part, you will find these places that have become supportive and more of them are opening each year.

Chapter 13: Looking Ahead: Colleges and Careers

Higher Education Opportunities

I interviewed Stephen Muller, the Director of Institutional Effectiveness of Landmark College, as well as some of his colleagues. Landmark College is a fully accredited Associate and Bachelor degree college exclusively for students with Dyslexia, ADHD, ASD, and other specific learning disabilities. Their class sizes range from as little as 3-4 kids per room, to a maximum of around 17 students. The average classroom size is around nine students.

Mr. Muller said, "The classes are 25 percent longer because of 'Point Of Performance Issues.'" Point of Performance Issues include executive functioning such as getting started on a project, being able to pace yourself, and knowing what is needed in order to complete a project. "Basically the kids need a lot of help getting organized."

"Our students come to us based on their cognitive abilities. Many of the kids have transferred from other programs. We are on a mission to help students succeed," a Landmark staff member exclaimed. "Our program includes satellite centers." Landmark has a writing center, math center, as well as others. They provide a 1-on-1 coaching staff and 1-on-1 coaching as in life coaching. "The vast majority of the kids go on to business and become entrepreneurs," Mr. Muller said. Some students major in other areas such as education and psychology. One other staff member chimed in with, "80 percent of our students over a six year longitudinal study receive a Bachelor's Degree." The school offers summer programs for high school juniors and seniors to try out their programs. "We are still a young place. In the future we are opening up a life sciences and computer gaming program," the staff exclaimed (Muller & Staff, 2012).

There are many colleges that accept special needs kids and provide services to help them pass their exams, which may such accommodations as providing taping devices or a person to help them study, library services, and so on. But there are few programs that are exclusively geared toward the special needs population. Thankfully, Landmark College is one of them. While originally Landmark was a 2-year college, they have already added Bachelor's Degree programs. That will qualify as a foundation for Graduate studies. The Landmark College has an Associate of

Science in Computer Science/Gaming that teaches interactive design, web design, 3-D development and game design. They have added cyber security and geographic information systems. It is modeled after, in some ways, the International Game Developers Association. So many of our autistic and ADHD children live by "gaming;" it is a natural place for them to create new games using their talents and abilities.

On February 9, 2012, I interviewed the Interim President of Beacon College, Dr. John Hutchinson. Beacon College has been fully accredited by the Commission Oncologists of the Southern Association of Colleges and Schools since 1989. Hutchinson said that Beacon is one of the only schools that was originally started by parents, which sets it apart from most other schools. Dr. Hutchinson says that psycho-educational evaluation and the diagnosis of a specific learning disability and or ADHD is looked at by the school when determining whether or not to admit a student to the college. "100 percent of our students either have a learning disability, ADHD, (Dyslexia), or a form of Autism," John said.

He continued, "We look to see if the student has the ability to do college-level work." While Beacon may take IQ into account with other evaluations, their admissions department is adept at assessing the student. "Each student is assigned a learning specialist. Then, each student gets a counselor. Lastly, each student is assigned a resident assistant (RA) who is trained as a life coach. Basically, this is a three-tier process," Hutchinson explained. If a family is having a hard time obtaining a quality

psycho-educational evaluation, that they can always come to Leesburg and the school can make a referral.

"The largest percentage of our students major in human services. Many go on for a Master's in social work, psychology, and counseling. Others go to work in community centers," John stated. When I asked if Beacon would consider hiring a person with disabilities, he said "We have recently hired a student who is now an admission counselor and another one for our IT department." The school is planning on opening-up a hospitality management program soon. They are also about to break ground on additional facilities. Dr. Hutchinson said that they accept approximately 60 percent of their applicants. "A large number of our students are transfer students. Those students have generally have failed in the mainstream and at other colleges. We put them back together again," Hutchinson excitedly exclaimed.

I asked him what happens if a student graduates the academic curriculum but seems not quite ready to enter the work force; I was so glad to hear that that situation is an issue Beacon has considered. They are working on a fifth-year transitional program. While the fifth-year students will not be living on the campus, they will receive an unpaid internship and classroom instruction. It breaks down into approximately 25 hours of work and 15 hours of classroom time. The program is expected to be at a greatly 'reduced fee' and the student is expected to live independently. But "we do not entirely cut them loose," Hutchinson added. He spoke of the possibility that the fifth-year transitional program would not only be for Beacon students, but for students from all over (Hutchinson, 2012).

Lately Beacon has been more competitive and more successful in recruiting. They tend to visit special schools and have recently been to Atlanta, Washington, and are on their way to San Francisco. Most people hear about Beacon on the Internet. Beacon is also open to expanding to other areas, and has considered the New England area, but for now, the priority is to finish building and open up the fifth-year transitional program. Hutchinson said that in some ways the school has been isolated and almost cut off from other areas.

My impression is that Beacon is a great institution to put your special needs student in, but I only wish there were many more places in addition to these few to choose from around the country to serve

Recovering Autism, ADHD, & Special Needs

our ever-growing special needs population.

Career Possibilities

Whether or not your child goes on to college, there are some decent career choices that can be considered, despite the fact the school system and society often leans toward getting the lowest and most menial forms of jobs for learning disabled and Autistic children. In fact, many high school programs are preparations for the one great day when the children graduate and become grocery baggers in supermarkets, floor moppers and table cleaners in fast food chains, and stock boys and girls in back room department stores. While there are a few high quality places such as the café in Tampa, Florida, called the Artistas Café (they call the Autistic baristas "Artistas"), which is run by Autistic youth and is in a Mercedes car dealership. It is a far better and more creative place to be than in a supermarket placing groceries in a paper bag for the rest of their lives. By working there, the goal is to have the kids become as independent as possible.

Many more such places are needed around the country that accommodate and promote the creativity and independence of the special needs population. I find that the companies that are mainly interested in getting the tax breaks to hire this population treat them rather poorly in general. There are many ongoing stories of these kids being laid off or fired because a different supervisor comes in or because of a misunderstanding in communication.

While there are always exceptions, I believe that with a little more creativity and ingenuity there can be an exciting world of places where the mid-range to severe autistic youth can do also well and develop skills. There are a host of careers in which they can be basically self-employed; what I mean by this is working in a manner where they do not have to punch in and out of a time clock. They are encouraged to set up a time schedule that works for them throughout their lives. For example, if they were not a morning person, a job that starts in the afternoon would be best suited for them. A schedule that is somewhat leaning toward part time and not full time hours – 25-30 hours or so – would be preferable than 40 hours a week. I am now going to offer some specific examples.

If your special needs youth has had a passion for growing plants as many do, a small greenhouse in which they might grow exotic plants on the wholesale level to resell to retailers might be an extraordinary career. This would be a perfect example of where a person could set up their own schedule by maintaining the plants in the afternoon rather than in the morning, and might be able to grow the plants without having to put in 40 hours a week. This would also be an area of freedom to be creative to the individual and self-empowering. The main issues would be that they could choose the time to water the plants, what to grow, they can come and go as they please without punching a clock, and they can control their environment. Can you just imagine a young person who has a nurturing love for plants like orchids or even Bonsais?

Another example might be to breeds or assist someone who raises dogs in the breeding of puppies. This takes a lot of work, but these kids will love their job.

Breeding would involve feeding, walking, socializing, and cleaning the animals. It might involve assisting in the delivery of the puppies on the delivery day and greeting customers as they come in to purchase the new puppies. These kids can also play with the puppies and get them collar-ready for a perspective buyer. If your young person loves animals, this would be a win-win situation. In fact, taking care of any animal, such as ferrets, aquarium fish, reptiles, and horses, would be a wonderful career path.

Why doesn't your child become a photographer or photography assistant? Holding the light, bringing in the equipment, giving a warm smile, and helping in the studio, are all things that can be done. Your youth may also learn how to take a portrait and make themselves present at events such as weddings.

Because there is a lot of non-verbal communication, this career would be ideal for a variety of affected young people. They might be able to study Photoshop and scrapbooking in order to improve their already-known skills, and better themselves so that one day they can do this for their clientele. These youth can excel very fast. If the child had a good voice, other positions would be an audio-book reader that records books on various media, announcers, and musicians.

For the very artistic Autistics, there is children book illustration, drawing comic strips, computer art, and blogging to other kids with special needs. Creating book covers for authors and publishers is in big demand.

Being a janitor is a great job, as well it is high paying and is completely decent as well as appropriate; it also provides many benefits (insurance, paid vacation, etc.). A quality control career in the manufacturing, packaging, and distribution sector that requires consistency is also to be considered because some are adept at noticing when something is done improperly.

There are certain jobs and positions at amusement parks that these young people can apply for. Some examples would be wearing character costumes, handing out balloons, and being greeters at certain restaurants and venues around the park. Some other jobs include being a camp counselor's assistant. Movie theaters have job openings from tickets to maintenance, popcorn makers, and so on. Also, running movie projectors or working in a bookstore, making sure the books are properly ordered and shelved. Operating a toy store is yet another good job option.

A person with Autism can work at a café learning the tricks of the trade by making coffees, smoothies and other drinks. Some children could become great bakers. They would truly enjoy the art of baking special goods. Some other jobs would be a waiter or waitress. The children would have the capability of taking down a food order, but it would also improve their social skills and social interaction with the public in time.

For those Autistics who enjoy and have a flare for fashion, working in a retail clothing shop is a good choice. They could keep items folded, assist in the dressing rooms, and also create window displays. Also, shoe and handbag repair. Some autistics absolutely can take on the career of becoming rental agents or assistants. They can open the doors of property and show it, make sure the lights are on and off, and make sure everything is as it should be.

Being a car detailer or bike mechanics can be considered as well. Any general maintenance such as light fixtures and putting together small furniture are good bets for jobs.

One other really great job would to become a librarian or librarian assistant. There are other jobs linked to the computer and are creative; one example would be someone who creates crossword puzzles or Sudoku. Also data entry work, inventory date, and designing restaurant menus, brochures, and flyers. Writing about Autism is becoming popular, too. You would be surprised how skillful and adept they can be at teaching or tutoring as an instructor or aid. With colleges opening online degrees with people with Autism, I anticipate that in the next 5-10 years from

now, there will likely be online teaching jobs opening up for members of the autistic community to teach.

Special Needs Characters in books and television

Special needs people have reached the point of being represented in popular mass media. One often sees depictions of people with Asperger's, the high functioning autism that the term "Rocket Scientists" would bring to mind. Geeks and nerds from the past may have fallen into that category. The best known and loved is the character of Dr. Sheldon Cooper, who plays the role of a theoretical physicist focusing on quantum mechanics and string theory on the show, "The Big Bang Theory." The character Dr. Sheldon Cooper is obsessed with his field, but must consistently eat a certain food and visit the comic stores only on specific nights.

Changing the schedule would put him into a panic. He lives by structure and he can not handle disruptions. He is unable to make transitions from one activity to another and is anal retentive about his likes and dislikes. And watch out if you sit on HIS spot on the couch. There have been other television shows that portray special needs characters. These include *Parenthood* (2010), which features a family that has to adjust to the difficulties of their Autistic son; *Boston Legal* (2004), the attorney Jerry Espenson is diagnosed with Asperger's in the third episode; and Dr. Spencer Reid on *Criminal Minds* (1994).

Also there have been various films where the main character was a special needs person. These films include: *I Am Sam* (2011), *What's Eating Gilbert Grape?* (1993), and the well known film *Forest Gump* (1994).

There are also some books that feature special needs characters for both adults and juvenile reading. Some of the best books I have ever read on the subject of children with special needs, their failures and triumphs, were actually written for children, by Caroline Janover. *Josh: A Boy with Dyslexia,* first published in 1988, is a book in which the author introduces Josh, a young boy who learns differently. This special character faces being teased and made fun of; his older brother is gifted and gets everything right. Josh remains disorganized and when we can't find his sneakers, he gets back at his brother for hiding them. He later pin pricks his brother's acne medication. The fact of the matter is that Simon, the older brother, did not hide Josh's sneakers, but they were just "mislapsed" (misplaced).

Janover's characters and their characteristics tend to go from book to book and reappear in *The Worst Speller in Junior High* (1995), and *Zipper: The Kid with ADHD* (1997).

Caroline Janover herself is dyslexic. "When I was in the second grade for the second time, my teacher told me to stand in the waste paper basket because my handwriting was all crooked and I read so slowly," Janover remembers. Although school was very difficult for her, she earned two masters degrees in Special Education; she attended Boston University, Sarah Lawrence College, as well as Farleigh Dickinson University.

One of the inspirations for writing her children's books is because both of her sons also had school difficulty and Dyslexia. Caroline states on a publishing website, "As as educator and author, I lectured to school children and educators all over the country about the importance of humor, hope, resiliency, and self-advocacy, especially when growing up with Dyslexia and ADHD."

I asked Caroline if her children, now grown, did well because she helped them through and taught them. She responded, "I was not their teacher. I certainly stood by and watched over their IEP's. It's important to understand children's strengths; that is hard because you want them to feel good about themselves." My interpretation of that statement is that when you're working with a special needs child, you want them to feel good about themselves, but they have issues when they might not be doing well. It's hard to keep a balance between wanting them to feel good about themselves and dealing with their issues.

Caroline said that she often sees kids who "weren't intelligent," but she knew that they were. Her first book *Josh: A Boy With Dyslexia* was rejected 56 times. Janover's book *The Worst Speller in Junior High* was rejected 48 times. That came as a complete surprise to me. For one thing, nearly every one of my students loved Janover's books. They easily related to the characteristics of the book's main antagonists and protagonists. Even some of my students who are not diagnosed with ADHD or Autism, but are average-but-struggling "C" students, enjoy and relate to the children and teens in the books.

Caroline went on to speak about a play she once wrote. During the play, it is the learning disabled and learning different child that rescues the grandfather who hurts his hip and falls into the water. The gifted and talented character does not do the rescuing.

The main thing that Caroline repeated as her main theme was "never give up!" Today, she concentrates on teaching at a private school, writing her memoirs, and working with parents. She sees many kids and teens that are a high level of functionality but have issues. She often asks kids what's worrying them and then works with their parents from that point on (Discussion of the research and teachings of Caroline Janover, 2012).

I personally find Caroline Janover's work to be a treasure chest that seems to have been become reburied over time. So many children today have learning disabilities or other issues, I would encourage teachers and other educators to take a fresh look at the body of this talented writer's work. How did this get lost in the shuffle? Her work is as relevant now as it was some 20 years ago.

Conclusion

The first large group of kids afflicted with Autism, ADHD, and other disabilities is just beginning to age-out of the public school system and programs that supported them when they were ill. From here on out, new roads must be paved that answers the question "What's next?" Parents and few experts are pioneering the majority of these new roads.

New resources will be opening that ask the question "Where will my child live when I am no longer able to take care of him or her?"; "Will he or she be able to be self-supportive in rough economic times?"; "Will my son or daughter find someone to love them, get married, and have children of their own?"; and "Will

my son or daughter be dependent on society, such as a group home?"

The author would like to point out that many of these kids could have successful careers, marriages, and families of their own. Some of the more ill ones may need supervision in their undertakings, especially for many of the ones who cannot communicate whatsoever. In the near future, I anticipate reviewing and working on special needs Internet dating websites, so I shall dedicate this chapter and rename it as "To Be Continued."

Appendix:
Articles Concerning Special Needs

Note: I have selected some of my previously published articles to be included in this section because your friends and family might be willing to read this whole book, but may be willing to instead at least read one or two specific articles that focus on particular special needs issues.

1 in 88 Children in the U.S. Now Have Autism... Or Is This The "New Math?"

The Center for Disease Control recently announced that 1 in 88 children in the United States now have Autism. Many were shocked at the escalation of Autism in the last few years, but some of us were shocked at the number. It seems inadequate to make this claim. The issue is that this number was based on children who were born in the year 2000 and were looked at in the year 2008. It was based on children who were eight years old in 2008 and it was handed to us as a "new" and latest finding in the spring of 2012. Therefore it was four years old by the time they released the information.

To my understanding it was based on children who were well enough to function in public school. Many children who cannot speak or wash themselves are in private school for Autism or not in school at all. Some lucky children with classic autism are homeschooled, and the less fortunate ones are institutionalized. This study left those children out of the numbers.

As aware as some of us think we are, most do not realize that pregnant mothers have been routinely vaccinated to prevent the flu. That is like vaccinating a fetus. Flu shots contain mercury under the name of *thimerosal*. The children who were vaccinated while still in the fetus stage were specifically not included in the 1 in 88, and I personally anticipate a large escalation from that factor alone.

What happened to the days when a pregnant woman had to ask her doctor if she could take so much as an aspirin because it might affect the fetus? According to the CDC, "To prevent influenza and complications in pregnant women, the Center for Disease Control and Prevention's Advisory Committee on Immunization Practices-ACIP- in 2004 began recommending routine immunization of pregnant women with the flu shot of any stage of pregnancy." They then claim that "Influenza Vaccine will protect pregnant women, their unborn babies, and protect the baby after birth."

Autism affects many more boys than girls. The ratio is between 5:1 and 4:1, depending upon which study you choose to rely on. The 1 in 88 equates to approximately 1 in every 54 boys, boys who were eight years old in 2008, now around the age of 12, well enough to be in public school. This means that children

from age 1-11 are NOT included in the rate.

The Center for Disease Control also found that the rate happens to be much higher in New Jersey. In New Jersey the number is 1 in every 49 children. This equates to approximately 1 in every 29 boys who are now 12 years old, and well enough to be in public school.

I am from the "Peanut Butter and Jelly Generation." We could eat peanuts and walk backwards at the same time. We had lights. Lots of lights attached to our 10 speed bikes. We rode out in the morning and came back at night using our bike mounted flashlights. We had Chicken-Pox, Measles, Mumps and no one in our community died from them. What we did NOT have was Autism. We had a few vaccines but did NOT get exposed to peanut by-products that have been added to vaccines since the United States passed a law that says we can never sue vaccine makers in regular courts in 1986. Consequently children went from a few vaccines to more than 70. Vaccine makers were awarded permanent immunity but children are not. Many children vaccinated with the Chicken-pox shot get Chicken-pox. Other sources claim that up to 81% of children who were vaccinated against Pertussis, Whooping Cough get Whooping Cough anyway. There is a difference between vaccination and immunization. There are a variety of articles I can quote but in the Clinical Infectious Diseases Journal, the title begins with "Unexpectedly Limited Durability of Immunity Following Acellular Pertussis Vaccination in Pre-adolescence in a North American Outbreak." Also in the news of

Smithtown, LI, 100% of the children with Whooping cough were fully vaccinated against it several summers ago.

When a "Peanut Butter and Jelly kid" got the Chicken-Pox they were protected and immunized for life. When today's children get vaccinated, it lasts for a few years then dissipates. Today's children require Booster shots over and over again.

As I wrote previously on this subject in the summer of 2010 in *"Childhood Has Become A Diagnosis Game,"* featured on the cover of the online Marci Magazine, a child's diagnosis of autism may depend on certain factors. A child in town "A" may receive a diagnosis of autism if the local public school has a good autism program. The same child with the same symptoms might be diagnosed with OCD, ODD, ADHD and numerous other mental illnesses in order to avoid the term autism because the local public schools might only have a "Learning Disability class," and not have a class for Autism. It seems that the doctors in the local districts tend to diagnose based on local school inquiries. I have seen children with co-morbid diagnoses and medicated Co-Morbidly. In sessions where I work with children 1 to 1 using art, teaching reading and writing, working with kids who have ADHD, Autism and Dyslexia, I have seen quite a few misdiagnosed. "When I get a new client, I might be told he is Autistic but might find NO Autism, rather, Dyslexia and high anxiety. Sometimes I am told the child just needs help with the grammar and sentence structure but turns out to have Asperger's syndrome or high functioning autism.

There is one more issue that is missing regarding this 1 in 88 number. I think that children with Asperger's Syndrome have been discounted because kids with Asperger's are high functioning. They usually do not get special education services. Think of little Sheldon Cooper-type children as depicted in the show, "The Big Bang Theory." If the child is autistic enough to get special education services, then they probably do not have Asperger's in the first place. He or she probably has a more classic form of autism. All this talk about autism having escalated because of better diagnosis and easier labeling ought to melt away once you realize what this supposed 1 in 88 might really mean. I long for the good old days when children caught a little virus and got over it instead of today's chronically ill children with Autism,

ADHD, OCD, dangerous food allergies, diabetes, depression and whatever else is going around. I believe that the truer number of Autism will mimic more closely the "1 in 6 children in the United States now have Developmental Disabilities."

Autism is Curable with Early Intervention

Question: I have always planned on homeschooling my children, and it was working out nicely with my seven year old. But my younger child is very disruptive, frequently screaming, crying, and can't sit still. So I've taken him to doctors and eventually to a psychologist for second opinions. Now I'm even more confused: one doctor said it's PDD-NOS (Pervasive Disability Disorder-Not Otherwise Specified), another's diagnosis is autism, the next said it was Asperger's Syndrome (high-functioning autism) and yet another says it's ADHD/ODD (Attention Deficit Hyperactivity Disorder/Oppositional Defiance Disorder). Can you help me make sense of this?

Shelley's answer: First let me say I'm sorry it is so complicated. Over the past decade and a half the diagnosis of PDD-NOS has been given across the board to countless children.

This is a catch-all phrase that covers a wide range of illnesses. It is an umbrella heading for ASD, meaning Autistic Spectrum Disorder that includes autism, and Asperger's Syndrome among other conditions.

The labyrinth of confusion begins when one takes a child like your younger one to a psychologist or psychiatrist in Town A, and the diagnosis is PDD-NOS.

Take the same child that same day to Town B, and you might be told that s/he has Asperger's Syndrome. And that's only part of it.

For example, even high functioning autism opens the door to an array of differing opinions: what one doctor describes as high-functioning, others do not.

Now take the same child, same symptoms, to Town C and you might be told that s/he has ADHD/ODD. Attention Deficit Hyperactivity Disorder combined with Oppositional Defiance Disorder.

If that is not confusing enough, within the next few years an estimated ten new diagnoses are anticipated. So eventually about every letter in the alphabet will be used!

Let's look at some practical solutions for your child regardless of the diagnosis:

1. If your child is not verbal, begin speech therapy IMMEDIATELY. This does not have to necessarily be ABA (Applied Behavioral Analysis) because there are many other effective methods out there.

2. If she/he falls a lot or is clumsy, begin physical therapy IMMEDIATELY.

3. If she/he cannot draw or paint, begin occupational and/or art therapy IMMEDIATELY.

4. Another avenue is Sensory Integration Therapy.

Try to get these services through your insurance, local school district, university, hospital or private therapy. Barter services if you have to i.e. hair-cutting, house-cleaning, healthy meals on wheels, piano lessons, etc. Do whatever it takes!

Time is of the essence, as I expressed in my August '08 article. This because a window of opportunity exists -- approximately between the ages of birth and five -- when the brain is flexible, and can regenerate, opening new, fertile pathways to cognitive and social skills.

So the good news is by starting early, you buy more time for your child with each intervention. And this window of opportunity can be extended even to the age of eight or nine!

As a parent you should accept your limitations and forgive yourself for having them. For example you may come to the conclusion that you will not able to home school your special needs child, and hire a special needs tutor. You need a break and let the preschool in your district provide services. Also, you and the rest of the family will need respite care and downtime.

But fortunately the sooner these services are in place, the better the child will get regardless of Alphabet City diagnoses. I have seen many young people with these disorders go on to live healthy independent lives. On the other hand I know children who have ended up in group homes or worse due to a lack of services, denial, and a lack of community support.

One success story is author Temple Grandin, who was diagnosed as autistic years ago. After obtaining her Ph.D. in the sciences, Grandin has designed small pens and round ramps that has changed the quality of life for millions of cattle around the world. Her family was relentless in getting her help after she was expelled from several schools and medical institutions. I highly recommend her books, and taped lectures in which she vividly describes the reasons for her childhood fits. These works bring logic to the issues these kids face.

All children with one or all of these diagnoses share certain traits: their sense of smell, sight, touch, and hearing is acutely heightened. If you find your child grabbing blankets and hiding under the table, building forts, or hiding in the closet, she/he is giving vital information. This is how you can learn what is needed to essentially cure your child.

These activities are actually forms of self-medicating. The fort reduces the light that might be overloading the child's system. The sound of the television may be like an explosion, therefore the fort, or closet muffles the noise.

If you put him in a sports program, imagine how the combined effects of the bouncing basketball, the view and echoing roar of the crowd, and florescent lights might seem to him: like "bombs bursting in air".

When you see her pulling off her shirt, the fabric is itchy to her, the tag digging into the skin. It's like sandpaper to her skin. He may need to wear the same colors every day and that is fine for now. Also, perfumes, soaps, cleansers, irritate him beyond imagination.

Certain textures in foods or colors can entirely disrupt her system. Any food dye with a number (i.e. red #5, blue #1, etc.) in such snacks as grape soda and cherry-flavored candy are made of tar and petroleum, which damage the functioning of the child. These poisons are used because they are cheaper than fresh fruits.

He may have food sensitivities to milk, soy proteins, wheat, gluten, etc. Sometimes even vitamins are not properly digested. Many of these children have skin problems like rashes and eczema.

Keep in mind that often it can be the gut interfering with the brain, rather than the brain interfering with the child.

All in all, autism is not one single illness, but a battery of multiple illnesses. The truth is that regardless of the diagnosis, as a parent you should do your best to deal with a WHOLE child, from soup to nuts. From their head to their toes.

Without question you have been dealt a hand that is very difficult. But I believe that a parent who wrote a question like yours has what it takes to solve the puzzle.

Suggested Reading: *MOTHER WARRIORS*, by Jenny McCarthy, author. Suggested DVD: *NORMAL PEOPLE SCARE ME*, produced by Joey Travolta (John's brother). Keri Bowers, author.

What do Autism, Music, Alzheimer's, and the DSM5 have in Common?

All three arenas are having their names and categories altered, two of them for the purpose of streamlining their definition in the DSM5. In the DSM5 (Diagnostic and Statistical Manual of Mental Disorders), put out by the American Psychiatric Association, the definition of what constitutes autism is about to be changed. Whole categories are to be removed by the psychiatric association. Terms such as Asperger's Syndrome and the PDDNOS (Pervasive Developmental Disabilities Not Otherwise Specified) are being removed from the DSM5; and they are coming under the axe in order to create supposedly less confusion. Many of us are aware that in essence, by un-diagnosing these kids, it may reduce services in education, health,

and other opportunities. Simultaneously, the same thing seems to be going on in the music industry.

The NARAS; National Academy of Recording Arts and Sciences, is attempting to drop 31 categories of music. The NARAS defended its actions by claiming that many categories were old and no longer represented a modern view of the music industry. According to Oscar Hernandez, a Grammy-winning member of the NARAS, this decision endangered many in the music industry.

Alzheimer's and autism are about to face the same fate; their lifespan is going to be shortened and streamlined just the like music industry. The definition for both is about to go into analysis and under the knife. Asperger's in plain English was the high functioning autism that the term "Rocket Scientists" would bring to mind.

283

Geeks and nerds from the past may have fallen into that category. Think Dr. Sheldon Cooper, who plays the role of theoretical physicist focusing on quantum mechanics and string theory on the show, "The Big Bang Theory." The character Dr. Sheldon Cooper is obsessed with his field, but must eat a certain food and visit the comic stores on Wednesday nights. Changing the schedule would put him into a panic. He lives by structure and he can not handle disruptions. He is unable to make transitions from one activity to another and is anal retentive about his likes and dislikes. And watch out if you sit on HIS spot on the couch.

The criteria for "Alzheimer's is about to be changed as well." Most people currently diagnosed with a mild form of Alzheimer's disease are about to be downgraded away from this term and re-

categorized as having MCI - Mild Cognitive Impairment. This is according to an article authored by Rachel Rettner found in *LiveScience.com* on February 6, 2012. The article goes on to say that people diagnosed as having 'Mild Alzheimer's disease' would be reclassified as having Mild Cognitive Impairment. MCI is recognized as an intermittent stage between "normal" loss of cognitive function that comes with age, and the development of Dementia. In essence they are changing and expanding the definition of Cognitive Impairment. It is a decline in cognitive functioning due to loss in memory and language, but does not interfere with everyday activities, yet reduces the Alzheimer's population.

According to the National Institute on Aging and the Alzheimer's Association, people with MCI can function independently. This could mean that even if people have some difficulties shopping, paying bills, and cooking but could still function, they would now be diagnosed as having MCI. Dr. John Morris, a professor of Neurology at Washington University School of Medicine, looked at people in a study and found that approximately 92% to 98% could be reassessed as having MCI and not Alzheimer's based on some tasks they were asked to perform including cooking and taking medication. This means that possibly 2 million people would have the diagnosis changed.

William Thies - chief medical and scientific officer of the Alzheimer's Association - says that the proposed changes to MCI are only around a year old and that Alzheimer's is a "…Continuum. We are trying to identify exactly where people will fit in the continuum of Alzheimer's." Where have we heard this before? It is nearly the same conversation that we are hearing regarding changing the definition of autism for the new DSM5. Autism Spectrum Disorders are also known as a *continuum*. The DSM5 proposes to streamline the definition to help clear things up and avoid confusion without taking responsibility for how that will affect numerous children across the country, not to mention other countries as well. Many schools for example already push parents to get a medical diagnosis in order to give their children more academic assistance. Special help for children struggling in academic areas was not designed to depend on a medical diagnosis, but in reality, schools have managed to make it appear this way to parents. Just like the proposed changes to the MCI are about a year old, so are the proposed changes to the DSM5.

Additionally, the proposed changes by the NARAS to remove categories in music are taking place as well. It seems that there is a far bigger picture here than what meets the eye. These three organizations are opting to streamline different definitions and different categories supposedly in an effort to benefit people. The truth is that it will eliminate help for many people, but line the pockets of the organizations. Take for example the people writing for the DSM5. When Asperger's and PDD is removed, schools will probably seek a "re-diagnosis" so that special education services could be restructured. Like everything else, the school budget is at risk and schools can no longer afford to have an abundance of services for the now 1 out of every 6 Developmentally Disabled kids or 1 out of 5 Neurologically Impaired kids. By changing the diagnostic criteria for autism, suddenly "POOF," large numbers of autistic children will magically disappear. Years and years of "better diagnosis" will bleed into un-diagnosis.

The revision that all 3 of these organizations are attempting to make is about money, period. Alzheimer's patients being redefined as having Mild Cognitive Impairment will probably no longer be eligible for the supervision of nurses or other insurance benefits. Many musicians will not be able to partake in the financial benefits of earning a Grammy Award particularly those in Jazz, Latin, and Hawaiian categories. Kids with PDDNOS will no longer meet the criteria necessary for health insurance or school to implement occupational, speech, or physical therapy. We have been seeing this pattern emerge in the health industry, but it has been occurring quietly in many aspects of life. Towns have been merging in order to share services and thereby save money. We have seen towns sharing police and fire departments, as well as administrative offices. We have been seeing different schools sharing child study teams. These shared services have not improved the quality of life. The benefits of saving money have not trickled-down to the individual.

Thies says that it is hard to tell the difference between MCI and early Alzheimer's. This is a dangerous slope in my opinion. Take for example the MCI guy who decides to make a breakfast consisting of eggs and a pot of tea. He turns on the stove and begins to cook. It is Sunday morning and he remembers that the *NY Times* was delivered to his front porch. He goes outside in pajamas and slippers, and forgets to take the key. Now, with the eggs cooking on the burner and the water boiling while the man is stuck outside, there is potential for the house to be in danger. At this very moment, it is Alzheimer's. MCI is the diagnosis, but the outcome of the forgetfulness sure has similar effects as Alzheimer's. By calling this MCI, he would not be eligible for certain assistance that a person with Alzheimer's could get such as part-time nurses to watch over him or certain therapies.

It appears that all this fancy footwork amounts to nothing more than a mere name game change. Changes are not always beneficial and children with autism will not go away. After all, a rose by any other name is still a rose.

Multiple Diagnoses Leading to Multiple Vials of Drugs

When we try to discuss or analyze things, there is usually a commonality in the language of what is being discussed. Take water for example, we all know what a glass of water is, clear, drinkable and comes from the earth. Sure, there are other perceptions such as the visualization or imagery of water from a babbling brook or water from an ocean, water from melting snow or water from a dew drop but we can still recognize the inherent nature of water.

There has become less and less commonality in the use of terms such as Autism, ADHD, OCD, PDD and the negative consequences seem to be rising rapidly. Today alone I heard from parents that their child is, "High functioning but bangs their head uncontrollably." That is not accurate. A child that persistently bangs their head is not high functioning, quite the opposite. Do the parents retort that because it makes them feel better? Did the doctor tell them that because insurance did not cover the fee and he or she wants to keep the client or ensure that they return for follow-up appointments?

When I hear that a child has ADHD, OCD and ODD, I cringe. Most of the time, I hear that the child is diagnosed with ADHD and Autism. This is an outrageous FAD. An ADHD child is hyperactive, on the run (Notable exception is while playing video or Magic Games.) disorganized, blows through homework, unable to check for errors when younger, and might be a little hyper -focused on cars or comics but when you tell them it is time to go somewhere-you might hear a whine or see a tear but the world does not come to a screeching halt and the rescue squad is not needed. Executive functioning including time management and planning is difficult. Socializing is difficult, making and keeping friends is an issue.

When the child is autistic, you might not be able to get them to transition from in the house playing to the outside without watching them exhibit tantrums or violent meltdowns, sometimes lasting for hours. Clothing creates serious problems; the young child will tear it off, bite or chew the sleeves, collars and shred the pants. Bathroom etiquette goes out the window and they often pee on the floor, in their beds, or in their pants until their teens. Food is as problem. The food can not be too mushy, crunchy or touch other foods. It is not like you can simply force feed them. They are prone to vomiting.

Speech is more often delayed and when they can not communicate screaming is a common sound. Most know

that some autistic kids do not learn to speak until adulthood or beyond. Some autistics bang their heads and self injure. They often hide under the table or in dark closets. Some do not respond to their name being called. Lining up toys, pots and pans is more intriguing than other activities.

While an ADHD child might prefer to line up cards or occasionally hide in a closet or have trouble with foods, individual symptoms are not earth shattering. But when it is autism functioning can grind to a halt. It is the propensity and severity of symptoms where we can clearly see the difference between autism and ADHD.

I do not understand how so many psychologically trained experts can confuse the two. In the area where I work now I have not seen one correctly diagnosed child, not one. It is an arena of

"Poly-diagnosis." Perhaps the doctors are multiply diagnosing the children so as not to miss something?

Has it become the norm to multiply diagnose because there is a list of symptoms on a page that gets checked off? Diagnosing kids is NOT a mathematical equation. It is not as simple as 1+1=2.

When I see a child with Autism, ADHD, OCD and ODD I am alarmed. When I see a child with ADHD and undiagnosed Learning issues I am equally concerned. More often a child with learning disabilities will behave in a manner that appears ADHD like or even autistic because he or she does not understand what is being taught in a classroom environment so they jump around, fidget or become destructive. Imagine if you were required to sit in a class 6 hours per day, 5 days per week in a room where only Cantonese is spoken. You would not be able to speak, read, write or contribute to the class. You might get angry, annoyed or display antisocial behaviors. Let's add to this hidden food allergies that most, nearly all of these children have. You do not necessarily need a diagnosis for this if your child gets severe intermittent bouts of constipation-diarea itchy skin, eczema, hives, constant croup, migraines and the like. These kids are sensitive to florescent lights, noise, perfumes and smells, cleaners, latex and rubber and a host of environmental sources. This seems to be what is missing in the psychiatry/ medical fields. This is exactly the point. When a child is ill, the entire child is ill. It takes someone who is able to maintain an open mind to discover how all of these factors affect the child synergistically, not in isolation.

The first thing to look at is: are the food related issues followed by chemicals and then begin with learning disabilities- not ADHD. So many diagnosed kids actually have Dyslexia or Dysnomia. It is not necessary to see a child reversing letters or numbers-after all Dyslexia is "A processing of information problem in the auditory, visual, or kinesthetic area. It is often confused with ADHD behaviors. It is as if what the child (or adult) learned is filed away in the brain. At a critical point the child can not find where they filed the word or information. He or she can practically see the word in their mind's eye but can not retrieve it. The next day they can retrieve it with ease when they do not have to as in a test. The dyslexic exhibits much of the same symptoms as ADHD or even Autism: disorganized, trouble with executive functioning, trouble following directions, and social skills issues. Their timing is off when trying to make or keep friends. They say things that are too brutally honest to others. They do not understand why people do not see the patterns that they see or the large picture at play. They are particularly adept at pointing out other peoples mistakes.

One of the reasons that experts seem to be losing sight of diagnosing kids is because of the push to put the child in a box where medication is deployed. It is to them a simple quick fix at a hefty price. It is not that medication is not helpful-it can be very helpful if a child has true ADHD, Not dyslexic, not autistic, not allergic to food or chemicals, not asthmatic and in this case the pill totally turns the child around in a few days without negative side effects- but good luck finding one of those. Even then when the first medication does not work they add another and another and another and sometimes the child gets worse. I saw a kid on 17 pills a day and that is considered progress? Zombies are not progress either.

Somehow we have come to see Autism / ADHD / OCD / ODD as a "Normal part of childhood. It is NOT NORMAL. Autism was extremely rare until the US passed a law in 1986 that stopped people from being allowed to sue a vaccine maker in regular courts and kids went from a few vaccines to more than 70...rapidly. By 1991 a shot was added to 3 hour old infants to prevent a sexually transmitted disease that they could not get unless they were shooting up with needles or the mother had it. Instead of blood testing the mother (. 0001% had it) - they opted to shoot all newborns and suddenly autism exploded.

Childhood diseases grew as did constant ear infections and many began to receive surgery in which ear tubes were placed; a bonanza for the medical community. Auditory processing issues rolled in. Speech OT PT therapies became serious careers. Constant antibiotics, once rare meningitis, flesh eating diseases and dangerous antibiotic strep throat was ushered in on the scene.

Getting back to the child diagnosed with PANDAS-Pediatric A Neurology it is becoming more prevalent but at it's core is sudden OCD Obsessive compulsive Disorder, washing hands hundreds of times per day, checking doorknobs excessively and sudden dangerous uncontrollable tics and Tourette's Syndrome. Recently renamed as PANS very few doctors are even willing to take a look at this phenomenon. This issue is so simple but not taught in medical schools. It is actually often Strep throat that lodges in the brain. Sometimes it is another Neurotoxin. Even Lyme disease can attack the brain. I hope by now you are beginning to see where I am going with this. These conditions are primarily medical –NOT psychiatric. The child banging his head might be trying to create a pain that he controls or knows that he generated rather than deal with the constant pain that he can not control, does not know where it came from. When throwing themselves over a couch or chair it might relieve the stomach pain by creating pressure.

Schools have accepted the overwhelming amount of ill children. Cafeterias have adjusted to the peanut allergy epidemic by creating peanut free zones and they are not interested in learning how peanut by products were added to vaccines thereby causing schools to make a major investment not in books but in Epi-pens, offering a drugstore of lunchtime medications faithfully delivered by parents to the nurses office complete with medical authorizations from pediatricians, neurologists, psychiatrists and divorce court orders when one parent wants the child to medicate while the other does not.

The United States consumes more than half of the medications available world wide. All other counties combined do not consume what we do. A FB friend studying to be an MD from Sweden once asked me "Are all the people in the US druggies?" I had to reply that most of us are. My belief is that the medications were set up due to the horrific amount of toxins our children have been shot up with. Aluminum, Thimerosal (mercury) embalming fluid, peanut oil, Squalene, Neosporin, ether, rats brains, dog kidney cells, aborted fetal tissue, parts of monkeys, cows pigs, caterpillars-delivered in multiple needles with latex, adjuvents… sounds yummy. Then there is the genetically modified foods created by the same companies that created DDT, Agent Orange, and other chemicals.

These compounds have sent a shockwave through our systems. Thus, a large amount of people are on antipsychotic medications, antidepressants, mood altering, plus Statins (cholesterol lowering), blood medications, either thinners or coagulants, diabetes medications, obesity medications, and medications for every situation or disease under the sun. Popping a pill or taking a drug has become as American as an apple pie.

Vaccine Requirements for School: Exemptions Allowed by Law

Vaccine requirements for school vary from state to state but in all states except two, there are religious or personal, philosophical or conscientious belief exemptions. By law, public schools must allow for the exemptions but religious private schools might not accept exemptions.

Mom & dad: Your child has rights and you should be aware of them

There are three basic facts you should remember when you are exercising your right to make an informed, voluntary vaccination choice for yourself or your child in America:

1. **Informed Consent is a Human Right:** The right to voluntary, informed consent to a medical intervention, including use of a pharmaceutical product such as a vaccine that can injure or kill you or your child, is a human right.

While the State may have the legal authority to mandate use of vaccines, nobody has the moral authority to FORCE you to get vaccinated or vaccinate your child without your voluntary, informed consent

2. **Vaccine Laws Have Exemptions:** In 1905, the U.S. Supreme Court affirmed the legal authority of state governments to pass laws requiring citizens residing in the state to use certain vaccines.

Today, all 50 states have enacted vaccine laws that require proof of vaccination for children to attend daycare, elementary, junior and high school and college.

Vaccine requirements vary from state to state and all 50 states allow a medical exemption to vaccination; 48 states allow a religious exemption to vaccination; and 18 states allow a personal, philosophical or conscientious belief exemption to vaccination.

To find out what your state vaccine law says and which exemptions you may take and how to take them, go to http://www.nvic.org/Vaccine-Laws/state-vaccine-requirements.aspx.

3. **Freedom is Not Free, Become a Vaccine Choice Advocate**: Many state governments now require nearly three dozen doses of more than a dozen vaccines to attend school. Medical and religious exemptions are becoming harder to get and exemptions for reasons of conscience are under attack by proponents of forced vaccination.

The National Vaccine Information Center is working with citizens in states to expand or protect legal exemptions to vaccination.

Exemptions are getting harder to get and it is downright confusing to most folks when they continually hear about new vaccine mandates. You are not getting the whole truth when you hear on the news or the radio that children will not be permitted to enter school without shots. Even people fully against vaccines still believe that their children must get them for school. On top of that notion there are

new vaccines entering the market at a rapid pace and people have no idea that some were licensed in the year 2000 though an increase of seizures, fevers and even 12 cases of death were realized before the vaccine was approved.

Five of the deaths according to an article by Dr. Mercola were counted as Sudden Infant Death Syndrome, SIDS. Something I almost never heard of prior to the new laws giving vaccine manufactures immunity from lawsuits if children died or seizured as a result of vaccines. It was pointed out that a pneumonia vaccine was tested against a meningitis vaccine and a real placebo was not used. This in my opinion is like testing a new diabetes drug up against a sugar pill. That actually happened. Parents do not realize that their baby started getting new pneumonia vaccines in the year 2000 at 2 through 15 months of age. Yet we all know by now that the number of autistic children has skyrocketed since 2000.

By contacting the National Vaccine Information Center, you can learn how to exempt your child in your state. I am never surprised at how many young parents contact the NVIC for a vaccine exemption for their SECOND child, once their first child seizured since getting vaccines. I am also not surprised at how many healthy, non-autistic, non-ADHD children there are in families where the first child was injured and the second child never received a vaccine. Families like that are on the front-line. The more they speak up, the greater chance that others will remain open to educating themselves as to vaccine ingredients, risks of vaccines and actually seek out healthcare providers that are not so "Trigger-happy."

Remember, at best, protection from disease by injections only lasts from several months to a few years, thus booster after booster must be received. A natural infection like Chickenpox lasts a lifetime. A vaccine injury can last a lifetime as well.

Individuals with Disabilities Education Act,

188, 198, 206

Infant Strokes, 21

inflammation, 104, 109, 110, 123, 129

intervention, 70, 78, 88, 173, 175, 187, 202,

279, 296

itchy skin, 43, 80, 84, 291

K

Know Your Rights in Special Education, 189,

197

L

Landmark College, 3, 224, 226, 257, 258

latex, 97, 117, 118, 140, 291, 295

Learning Disabilities, 7

Least Restrictive Environment, 207

Leonardo Da Vinci, 94

M

Mainstreaming, 208, 217

Mathematical Disorder, 8, 31

Mayo Clinic, 81, 97, 104, 105, 112

Melatonin, 67, 79, 170

mercury, 8, 11, 29, 56, 121, 122, 123, 124,

125, 127, 134, 273, 294, 300

Mercury, 122, 124, 125, 300

mineral oil, 137

mold, 85, 97, 103, 117

Mortality Graphs, 24

MSG, 8, 17, 18, 19, 20

Munchausen by Proxy, 39, 40

Music therapy, 180

N

National Childhood Vaccine Injury Act, 9

National Institute of Mental Health, 227

National Vaccine Information Center, 3, 26,

297

END NOTES

[i] Numeric figures used in this chart were accessed on November 29, 2011, 12:19 p.m. from http://en.wikipedia.org/wiki/Diagnostic_and_Statistical_Manual_of_Mental_Disorders

[ii] See a video related to this concept as well as several other ideas presented in the book at http://holisticremediesnews.com/2684/conquering-developmental-problems-in-children/

[iii] The ingredients of these shots have been known to change on a regular basis, and may not be 100% accurate as per today's contents.

[iv] See Dr. Eisenstein's webinar archives for 2009 via http://homefirst.com/ for more information on strokes related to vaccines

[v] According to their website found at http://www.sunyopt.edu/, the mission statement of the center "is to provide support for vision science research, patient care and scholarships and fellowships at the College and its clinical facility, the University Optometric Center. The foundation also promotes scholarly development in vision science and public health education in vision and sight development.
Underscoring its mission is the commitment by the Board of Trustees of the foundation to support outreach community programs for underserved men, women and children in need of vision care" (OCNY 2011).

[vi] More information and examples can be found at http://www.eyecanlearn.com/

[vii] To see more about the Gluten Free/Casein Free Food List and for information about how to start the diet and how it benefits Autism, visit The GFCF Diet Intervention website at http://gfcfdiet.com/beginningthediet.htm

[viii] See the last page of The ARI Mercury Detoxification Consensus Position Paper. The last page of the paper contains a copy of the Mercury Detoxification Evaluation Form (MDEF). This form is designed to allow parents to track how well their child is responding to a mercury detox procedure. The MDEF score reflects the severity of the child's symptoms.

[ix] Chelation is not new and has been used successfully in the 1970s for individual cases for people affected by poisons, but today there is a large portion of a generation of children that need chelation across the board.

[x] See more information about this in the Food and Drug Administration study entitled "Update on Bisphenol A for Use in Food Contact Applications: January 2010." Which can be found online at http://www.fda.gov/newsevents/publichealthfocus/ucm197739.htm

[xi] As was documented in Liz Szabo's article "Bisphenol A: What You Need to Know" found in USA Today, accessed via http://www.usatoday.com/news/health/bpa.htm

[xii] More information can be found on the properties of Mullein Oil in Back to Eden, 1998, p. 181. They describe Mullein Oil as something that was regularly used for childhood illnesses.

[xiii] The Optometric Center of New York is located at SUNY College of Optometry's University Eye Center on 33 West 42nd Street in New York, New York. More information about them can be found at http://sunyopt.edu/uec/ or by calling their hotline at (212) 938-4001.

[xiv] A useful resource for finding out more about Section 504 exists at the following webpage: http://www.greatschools.org/special-education/legal-rights/868-section-504.gs

[xv] For a complete list of terms, head to: http://www.understandingspecialeducation.com/special-education-terms.html

[xvi] An interesting article discussing this idea of a school being right for one child but not for another can be found at http://seattletimes.nwsource.com/html/health/2015578833_autistic14.html

[xvii] Information about Landmark College and the learning resources they offer can be found on their website at

http://www.landmark.edu/ld-and-adhd-resources/

[xviii] Alternatively, check out http://www.defeatAutismnow.net/ to find more information about IEP's, therapy, and general advice regarding Autism.

[xix] This article can be found online at http://issuu.com/joannadg/docs/marci_summer_0621111issuefix

[xx] For more information about the Canary Party, How to recover a vaccine injured canary, and what it means to be a Canary in a coalmine, visit http://www.canaryrecovery.com/

[xxi] For a description of the disability-specific programming offered in both the winter and summer, go to http://www.adaptivesports.org/ and check out Summer Programs, Winter Programs, and Participant Info.

[xxii] Find this organization at http://www.dolphins.org/